ENDURING
THE
REFINER'S FIRE

OTHER COVENANT BOOKS AND AUDIOBOOKS
BY DAVID T. MORGAN

My God Hath Been My Support:
Seven Keys to Understanding and Enduring Personal Trials

ENDURING THE REFINER'S FIRE

EMOTIONAL RESILIENCE FOR LATTER-DAY TRIALS

DAVID T. MORGAN, PhD

Covenant Communications, Inc.

Cover image courtesy istockphoto.com

Cover design copyright © 2022 by Covenant Communications, Inc.

Published by Covenant Communications, Inc.
American Fork, Utah

Copyright © 2022 by David T. Morgan
All rights reserved. No part of this book may be reproduced in any format or in any medium without the written permission of the publisher, Covenant Communications, Inc., P.O. Box 416, American Fork, UT 84003. This work is not an official publication of The Church of Jesus Christ of Latter-day Saints. The views expressed within this work are the sole responsibility of the author and do not necessarily reflect the position of The Church of Jesus Christ of Latter-day Saints, Covenant Communications, Inc., or any other entity.

Printed in the United States of America
First Printing: January 2022

28 27 26 25 24 23 22   10 9 8 7 6 5 4 3 2 1

ISBN 978-1-52442-095-6

ACKNOWLEDGMENTS

I FIND IT NO SURPRISE that the idea for this book came at the beginning of the COVID-19 pandemic. Once I had become convinced that "two weeks to flatten the curve" was going to extend into months or longer, I knew I had to do something different with my life. I couldn't simply hold on and resume as normal; things were going to change. It was up to me whether they changed for the better or for the worse. Writing this book has helped me examine my life and truly question whether I am enduring well or merely enduring. COVID-19 isn't my first storm and won't be my last. I'm grateful for the scriptures, the words of modern Church leaders, and the inspiration of the Holy Ghost, which have helped me along the way. I'm truly grateful to my parents and siblings, who have weathered their own storms and taught me ways of endurance and fortitude that I could not have learned on my own.

I have been greatly blessed by many friends who have willingly sacrificed of their time to refine and polish my rough ideas. I'm thankful for Deena Morgan, Sharyle Karren, Janet Petersen, Dianne Esplin, Sharon Cross, Marilyn Harker, Janae Smith, and Barbara Rogers for their reviews. I'm very thankful to Bonnie Brien, who has provided indispensable support by way of editing and organization. I'm grateful to Kami Hancock, Michelle Pipitone, Amy Parker, and the rest of the team at Covenant Communications for their help in getting the manuscript and cover ready for publication and being willing to distribute it to the world. I love and appreciate my children and grandchildren, who are a constant source of inspiration and support. And I'm most grateful for my amazing wife, Kristyn, who has been with me from the beginning to the end of this process. She is my rock and my greatest happiness.

TABLE OF CONTENTS

Foreword viii
Preface xi
Author's Note xiii
Chapter One: The Furnace of Affliction 1
Chapter Two: The Blessings of Disruption 9
Chapter Three: Understanding Identity and Purpose 19
Chapter Four: The Savior's Enabling Power 27
Chapter Five: Personal Competence 37
Chapter Six: Tenacity 49
Chapter Seven: Acceptance of the Strengthening Effects of Stress 61
Chapter Eight: Tolerance of Negative Affect 73
Chapter Nine: Accepting Change 85
Chapter Ten: Building Secure Relationships 99
Chapter Eleven: A Sense of Control 111
Chapter Twelve: Increasing Spirituality 123
Appendices 134
About the Author 159

FOREWORD

I MET DR. DAVID MORGAN a few years ago as we shared the platform doing virtual firesides for Onward Productions. Over the years I've watched him help people fight and battle courageously through challenging circumstances that would give most of us reason to surrender and quit. David does this with unwavering passion! He personifies endurance because he understands that those with it DO, while those without it try.

In this masterfully written book, David paints a picture of proven principles to help us endure some of the most agonizing seasons of life. His life experiences marinated with powerful storytelling give us a unique perspective on how to endure the refiner's fire. Within these pages David reveals that it is in our darkest hours that we often discover our life's purpose. He has a way of taking you to that special moment in your life wherein your truest dreams and aspirations stir. He will challenge your intentions and encourage you to evaluate and define your finest hour.

With humor and compassion, David authentically inspires those who are emotionally paralyzed by worry, fear, or doubt and falsely believe they have little to contribute. When we surrender our resistance to change and growth, we release the brake that is often holding us back. This is when you have to get real; it is when you have to be honest and be willing to face the fear that holds you bound.

The real blessing and beauty of healing, both emotional and physical, comes from becoming stronger than you were before the injury or the circumstance that created the injury. It is true that a broken bone heals twice as strong. David describes how our purpose can never fully be realized without the pain and fear we each must work through and that our potential could not be reached without our learning the value of setting goals worthy of suffering for. He also teaches us to be grateful for what we DO have, not what we don't have, and to focus on the possible, not the impossible.

These principles of truth will inspire you to live your own life to its fullest. When circumstances seem too hard, or when life feels hopeless or unfair, you will be equipped with the necessary tools to shift your focus to what you can do instead of what you can't do. If you are feeling stressed because of crushing burdens or are overwhelmed with too much to do or too much to overcome, this book is for you. David reveals essential truths and wisdom that will place you squarely back on your path and purpose.

I have seen David move an audience of thousands to tears as they connect with the power of their God-given potential. David has this unique ability to lift and raise the sprits and hopes of those burdened with despair and heartache. He has shared a rare gift in teaching us to conquer heartbreak and doubt by enduring to succeed, not just in spite of our challenges but because of them. The message and wisdom contained in the pages of this book will invite infinite possibilities into your life.

It has been said that "Every thought we think is creating our future. . . . The thoughts we think and the words we speak create our experiences."[1] Dr. David Morgan is an extraordinary example of one who knows that what we believe about ourselves defines our destiny and that our dreams are destroyed not by our circumstances but by our beliefs.

Take the leap into these pages and find yourself immersed in incredible wisdom!

—Chad Hymas, CSP, CPAE Leadership Speaker Hall of Fame

---

1 Louise Hay, *You Can Heal Your Life* (Carlsbad, CA: Hay House, Inc.), 2004, 1.

PREFACE

I DISTINCTLY REMEMBER THE SECOND week of March 2020. I was traveling for business in Washington state. For a couple of months there had been news of a new virus that originated in China, but the impact in the United States had been nothing more than a few talk show monologue jokes and funny memes. That week was a little different, as the effects of the virus started to hit home. As I visited a government office for business, they were limiting the number of people who could be in the waiting room at any given time. *No worries*, I thought. *This is just a precaution that probably won't result in anything serious.* How wrong I was.

Within forty-eight hours, our governor had effectively declared a state of crisis. All public schools were closed. Government offices were shuttered, which meant a large portion of my business was temporarily on hold. In-person Church meetings were canceled. My wife had to make a hurried and unplanned trip to Idaho to retrieve our son from college, as his classes had shifted to being fully online. Our state imposed a stay-at-home order, in which all nonessential businesses were closed. Supermarket lines snaked for blocks as we lined up, six feet apart, to stockpile cleaning supplies and toilet paper. The sudden changes were dramatic, and the anxiety was palpable. As my personal fears increased, I sought for reassurance by creating my own narrative that these conditions would probably last only a couple of weeks. Again, how wrong I was.

Now I sit here, almost one year later, writing this account. Most businesses have reopened, and many people are back to work. Our state requires us to wear masks in all public buildings. Our in-person Church meetings have not resumed. Summer break has come and gone, and public schools are now online. COVID-19 infection rates have stabilized in some parts of the world, but in others they continue to spike. This invisible threat still causes me to be cautious about contact with others. The pandemic has become a political issue, and there are varying opinions regarding its overall level of dangerousness. Regardless of one's personal beliefs about COVID-19, it is impossible to ignore the devastating effect it has had on individuals and economies worldwide. To be frank, this is the most serious, far-reaching, and longest-lasting stressor I have experienced in over fifty years of life.

Why do I tell you this experience? This global contagion has created a veritable barometer to measure emotional strength in both myself and everyone I know. All of us have been pressed to our limits. Some people have risen above and become stronger. Others have struggled. My own journey has varied between these two extremes. I have discovered areas of personal weakness and simultaneously found that my capacity to endure stress is stronger than I thought it was. Above all, I have been able to develop a deeper dependence upon God, truly having to trust in Him. Throughout this entire ordeal, I've maintained an underlying belief that not only will things eventually work out but they will also be better than before. It has been hard to sustain that assurance as days turn into months and years, with little hope on the horizon. Yet that beacon of faith that all will be well remains constant, keeping me going day-to-day. I'm profoundly grateful for that.

Emotional resilience is an important topic that has become more salient as adversity seems to be on the rise. COVID-19 and its variants have been a stressor of global proportion, but whether challenges are small or global, we have always endured them at an individual level. As time has rolled on and society has progressed, these difficulties have changed in form. For most, gone are the days of building homes from logs and farming to get food. Housing is available. Transportation is modern and convenient. Obtaining food is as simple as walking into a grocery store, where thousands upon thousands of options are there for the purchasing. Most of us no longer have the same worries as our forebears. But I believe our emotional stressors are as significant as they ever have been. I think mental and emotional difficulties just might be the signature challenge of the twenty-first century. But an all-knowing and ever-loving Father in Heaven has prepared us for these troubled times by providing gospel-focused tools we can use to "endure it well" (D&C 121:8).

AUTHOR'S NOTE

I UNDERSTAND THAT THOSE WHO read this book will likely fall into many different categories. Some will already have good emotional resilience, and this will be a refresher course for them. Others will have few resilience skills but will be eager and ready for the challenge to improve. And there will be those who believe they desperately need greater emotional resilience but feel like they barely have the energy or resources to make it through the day, much less embark on a course of personal improvement. Reading a book such as this can leave some feeling exhausted and hopeless rather than motivated and hopeful. Please allow me to address that third group for a moment.

You are remarkable. So many of you have been through extremely difficult trials that have left you bruised and broken. Yet you have survived and endured. You continue to move forward as best you can. That is no small feat, and you should be proud of your efforts. You are stronger than you think you are. Even the fact that you have this book in your hands and are considering reading it suggests you have a willingness to improve. All journeys begin with one step. Try not to fault yourself for what you perceive as slow progress; give yourself credit for all forward movement. There are no deadlines for spiritual improvement. The Lord is more merciful than we can possibly imagine. He does not look for ways to cut us off or call out, "Time's up!" as if we are taking some standardized test. He loves us. He loves you. He wants you to succeed. He will do everything He can to make that possible. You get credit for the things you do in addition to the things you *want* to do. "For I, the Lord, will judge all men according to their works, *according to the desire of their hearts*" (D&C 137:9; emphasis added). The Savior knows our weakness, knows our hearts, and will bless us as abundantly as possible as we strive to keep His commandments.

I truly desire for this book not to leave you feeling overwhelmed. I want you to feel hopeful—hopeful about your future, hopeful about your potential, and hopeful that with the Savior's help, you can accomplish many great things. If you feel you are too far gone or have too little ability to make even the first step toward greater emotional resilience, I recommend the words of Elder Jeffrey R. Holland:

> However late you think you are, however many chances you think you have missed, however many mistakes you feel you have made or talents you think you don't have, or however far from home and family and God you feel you have traveled, I testify that you have *not* traveled beyond the reach of divine love. It is not possible for you to sink lower than the infinite light of Christ's Atonement shines.[2]

Might I also add that you have *not* traveled beyond the reach of divine help. Whatever struggle you have, whatever setbacks you've experienced, they can all be helped and healed through the Savior's magnificent power. I believe that with all my heart.

As you begin this study of emotional resilience and gospel doctrines, take courage. Don't run faster than you have strength, but strive to be diligent (see Mosiah 4:27). If you aren't strong enough now to do some of the exercises or incorporate some of the principles, that's okay. Don't worry about what others are doing or how your efforts compare to theirs. Do your best every day. Some days your best may result in no apparent progress at all, as you simply tread water to survive. That's perfectly fine. Other days you may be able to do a little more. Give it your best shot and pray diligently for additional strength. I testify that the Lord will hear and answer your prayers. With genuine effort and in due time, you will begin to see personal improvement. God bless you as you sincerely strive to become like Him.

---

2 Jeffrey R. Holland, "The Laborers in the Vineyard," *Ensign*, May 2012, 33.

CHAPTER ONE
THE FURNACE OF AFFLICTION

Many are familiar with the story of Alma the Younger and the sons of Mosiah. They were a disobedient, troublemaking bunch until an angel called them to repentance. With that initial intervention, followed by years of repentance and change, they became incredible servants of the Lord. The sons of Mosiah decided their best possible service would be in the mission field. They pled with their father to permit them to serve among the Lamanites. After receiving heavenly reassurance that their lives would be spared, Mosiah sanctioned their proposal. Ammon, Aaron, Omner, and Himni left the safety of their home and went to their enemies, hoping to bring them to the light.

Ammon's story is practically famous among members of The Church of Jesus Christ of Latter-day Saints. If we were to look at his "missionary journal" for the first few weeks after he arrived in his first area, the highlights would read something like this:

- Got in to see the king
- Given an opportunity for marriage but declined it
- Was assigned to feed the sheep
- Defended the sheep at the waters of Sebus (chopped off a bunch of arms too)
- Taught the king and all of his royal court
- King passed out for three days; taught his wife during that time
- King and queen accepted the gospel, launching an avalanche of converts
- Rode in the king's chariot, met the king's dad along the way, and got a new referral

I'm not sure about most people's full-time missionary experience, but my first few weeks as a missionary were not nearly as successful. Ammon's situation was unique. We don't hear nearly as much about his brethren during that same period of time. Most of their account is found in just two verses: Alma 20:29–30. Based on these scriptures, the "missionary journal" of Ammon's brothers during those weeks would look something like this:

- Tried to preach to the people; they rejected us
- Went to another group of people; they rejected us
- Tried yet another group; they rejected us and then beat us up
- Were chased out of several towns; arrived in Middoni
- Were tied up and thrown into prison in Middoni
- Eventually rescued by Ammon and his new convert

We know righteous behavior does not prevent mortal suffering. That truth is manifest throughout scripture, with Aaron, Omner, and Himni being a case in point. Trial and tribulation can be very effective teachers, particularly if endured well, yet everyone responds to difficulty in different ways. Contrast the examples of the sons of Mosiah with those of Laman and Lemuel. Both sets of children came from privilege. Both sets of children had righteous parents. Both sets of children had heavenly manifestations that left little room for doubt. Yet these two groups went in very different directions. It is interesting to note that they both received visits from an angel commanding them to change their ways. Without constant cajoling, Laman and Lemuel wanted to give up and return to Jerusalem, sacrificing their opportunities for growth. Instead of looking forward with faith, they persistently looked back on comfortable pleasures not available in the desert. Indeed, they complained to Nephi, "Behold, these many years we have suffered in the wilderness, which time we *might* have enjoyed our possessions and the land of our inheritance; yea, and we *might* have been happy" (1 Nephi 17:21; emphases added). In their minds, suffering precluded their ability to be happy, yet the gospel teaches that we can find ways to be happy *despite* our sufferings. Aaron, Omner, and Himni were chased, mocked, beaten, and incarcerated. Surely that would have been ample reason to abandon what so many of their peers had considered a fool's errand in preaching to the Lamanites (see Alma 26:23–24). But they continued faithful, looking forward with hope toward better days.

The sons of Mosiah experienced considerable emotional turmoil but still persisted in faith. Ammon described their sufferings as follows:

> Now when our hearts were depressed, and *we were about to turn back*, behold, the Lord comforted us, and said: Go amongst thy brethren, the Lamanites, and bear with patience thine afflictions, and I will give unto you success. And now behold, we have come, and been forth amongst them; and we have been patient in our sufferings, and we have suffered every privation; yea, we have traveled from house to house, relying upon the mercies of the world—not upon the mercies of the world alone but upon the mercies of God (Alma 26:27–28; emphasis added).

Note how he remarks they were "about to turn back." Perhaps there were days they felt they had reached their emotional limits. How much suffering could they endure for a people who actively rejected them? If they were patient in suffering, however, the Lord's promised success was impending. In the end, He absolutely fulfilled His promise. Their converts, eventually known as the Ammonites, were one of the most faithful groups of saints in the entire Book of Mormon.

I have often heard people say, "Why would a loving God allow His children to suffer?" It is a reasonable question, particularly for those who are not religious or who have limited spiritual understanding. If suffering and adversity played no part in our eternal development, then a loving God would likely never allow His children to experience pain or grief. He would rescue at every moment, cradling them in celestial peace and comfort. But our Father in Heaven knows His purpose. It is to bring to pass our immortality and eternal life (see Moses 1:39). In order to become like Father in Heaven, we need repeated opportunities for purification and strengthening. This process is sometimes referred to as the "furnace of affliction" (Isaiah 48:10). Such experiences can be painful and difficult, so much so that some are often tempted to avoid them altogether. Isaiah wrote how ancient Israel desired the comfortable way, despite that path's low potential for progress: "Which say to the seers, See not; and to the prophets, Prophesy not unto us right things, speak unto us smooth things, prophesy deceits: Get you out of the way, turn aside out of the path, cause the Holy One of Israel to cease from before us" (Isaiah 30:10–11). In other words, the people of Israel pleaded, "Don't tell me things are going to be difficult; don't ask me to make significant sacrifices. Give me a smooth road with convenient choices." But the so-called "smooth roads" almost always lead to uninspiring ends. As the familiar saying attributed to motivational speaker Zig Ziglar goes, "Difficult roads often lead to beautiful destinations."[3]

As noted previously, adversity is a critical part of our existence. No one will get through life without a certain degree of difficulty. The righteous are far more likely to experience opposition and challenge, if only because this seems to be one of the best ways to develop spiritual strength. Avoiding adversity is not the goal. The goal is learning how to deal effectively with challenges. As we develop greater emotional endurance, we increase in capacity to withstand suffering and trials. We develop improved coping skills. And most importantly, we eventually become transformed from lesser creatures to ultimately achieve "the measure of the stature of the fulness of Christ" (Ephesians 4:13).

The October 2020 general conference of The Church of Jesus Christ of Latter-day Saints was held during the COVID-19 pandemic. As the pandemic dragged on for months and months, people talked about developing a "new normal" in their approach to everyday life. President Russell M. Nelson commented about this in his closing remarks: "The challenge for you and me is to make certain that each of *us* will achieve his or her divine potential. Today we often hear about 'a new normal.' If you really want to embrace a new normal, I invite you to turn your heart, mind, and soul increasingly to our Heavenly Father and His Son, Jesus Christ. Let that be *your* new normal."[4] Trials and other hardships hopefully help us become more like our Savior Jesus Christ. Viewing adversity as a stepping-stone for growth can help us achieve greater emotional resilience, if simply for the fact that we will see the value in such challenges.

One of the main purposes of life is to test our faithfulness. "And there stood one among them that was like unto God, and he said unto those who were with him: We will go down, for there is space there, and we will take of these materials, and we will make an earth whereon these may dwell; And we will prove them herewith, to see if they will do all things whatsoever the Lord their God shall command them" (Abraham 3:24–25). While trials vary in intensity, difficult tests often provide valuable information regarding who we are and what we can endure.

Consider the example of Abraham, the prophet of old. After being promised amazing blessings that would extend to his posterity (see Genesis 17:4–8), he and his wife Sarah were still childless. Following almost one

---

3 Zig Ziglar (@TheZigZiglar), "Difficult roads often lead to beautiful destinations," Twitter, April 17, 2017, 3:00 p.m., twitter.com/thezigziglar/status/854077020132847620?lang=en.
4 Russell M. Nelson, "A New Normal," *Ensign*, November 2020, 118.

hundred years of life, the Lord told Abraham and Sarah they would bear a child. This was the answer to decades of prayer and provided enhanced meaning to the blessings of the Abrahamic covenant. Fast-forward a few decades, when their only child, Isaac, was now a faithful and true follower of God. Surely his parents were incredibly proud of him. Abraham received another revelation regarding his son, this one in stark contrast to the one received decades earlier. The Lord commanded Abraham to kill Isaac in a ritual and holy sacrifice. Those who have truly loved someone can appreciate the gut-wrenching experience Abraham and Sarah must have gone through at that time. Fortunately, this story had a happy ending, but not until the bitter end. At the very moment when Abraham was about to take his son's life, an angel appeared and commanded him to refrain. Clearly this had been a test for Abraham, Sarah, and Isaac, and they all remained faithful throughout. In referring to this story, President M. Russell Ballard tells of a conversation between Elder Hugh B. Brown and Truman G. Madsen:

> Sacrifice allows us to learn something about ourselves—what we are willing to offer to the Lord through our obedience. Brother Truman G. Madsen tells about a visit he made to Israel with President Hugh B. Brown, an Apostle of the Lord who served as both Second and First Counselor in the First Presidency. In a valley known as Hebron, where tradition has it that the tomb of Father Abraham is located, Brother Madsen asked President Brown, "What are the blessings of Abraham, Isaac, and Jacob?" After a short moment of thought, President Brown answered, "Posterity."
>
> Brother Madsen writes: "I almost burst out, 'Why, then, was Abraham commanded to go to Mount Moriah and offer his only hope of posterity?' It was clear that [President Brown], nearly ninety, had thought and prayed and wept over that question before. He finally said, 'Abraham needed to learn something about Abraham.'"[5]

Significant tests lead to significant insights. Quite frankly, the greater and longer lasting the trial, the more potential for spiritual growth and personal sanctification. Yet the ability to endure varies from person to person. Why

---

[5] M. Russell Ballard, "The Law of Sacrifice," *Ensign*, October 1998, churchofjesuschrist.org/study/ensign/1998/10/the-law-of-sacrifice?lang=eng. Accessed October 16, 2020.

can some manage grief after grief, still striving to do their best, while others struggle to bear the burden? The answer is that there are psychological and emotional characteristics that contribute to strong coping abilities. These characteristics can be summarized within the framework of emotional resilience.

The concept of emotional resilience has been addressed in psychological literature for decades. It is important to understand what emotional resilience is and why it is a critical element in strong mental health as well as spiritual functioning. This chapter addresses some of the research history and academics associated with this concept. Without getting bogged down in a technical scientific discussion, I hope to illuminate some of the details of the overall conceptual structure. The following are some definitions of emotional resilience (often simply called "resilience" in professional literature) that help explain the construct. They are summarized in a review of resilience research authored by Isyaku Salisu and Norashida Hashim, as follows:

DEFINITIONS OF RESILIENCE[6]

Authors/Year	Definitions
Cheshire, Esparcia & Shucksmith, 2015	Individuals' ability to adapt to and recover from disturbing events
Hobfoll, Stevens & Zalta, 2015	The ability of individuals or human systems to absorb stressors and return to their original state when that stressor is lifted without creating permanent damage or harm
Everly Jr., Strouse & McCormack, 2015	The ability to see yourself in the dark abyss of failure, humiliation or depression—and bounce back not only to where you were before but to even greater height of success, happiness, and inner strength
Ledesma, 2014	The ability to bounce back from adversity, frustration, and misfortune
Connor & Davidson, 2003	Personal qualities that enable one to thrive in the face of adversity

---

[6] Isyaku Salisu and Norashida Hashim, "A Critical Review of Scales Used in Resilience Research," *IOSR Journal of Business and Management*, April 2017, table 1 on p. 24. (The table in this text represents only a portion of the source table.)

There are two major themes among these various definitions. The first theme is the idea that resilient individuals manage adversity effectively. The second, and possibly more important, theme is that resilient individuals become stronger as a result of adversity. Personally, I like the Connor and Davidson definition—"personal qualities that enable one to *thrive in the face of adversity*"—because it succinctly incorporates both of these major themes and is also consistent with gospel teachings. Mortality is a period of testing that involves struggle and difficulty (i.e., *experiencing adversity*). One of the main purposes of that testing is to change our very natures to become more like our Heavenly Father and the Savior (i.e., *thriving in the face of adversity*). Linda S. Reeves, former Second Counselor in the Relief Society General Presidency, stated,

> The trials and tribulation that we experience may be the very things that guide us to come unto Him and cling to our covenants so that we might return to His presence and receive all that the Father hath.[7]

The "personal qualities" Connor and Davidson refer to are beams and foundations that fortify our characters. They also provide needed structure as we hold fast to covenant promises during challenging times.

Researchers have determined distinct categories that define emotional resilience. There are several sets of definitions, all somewhat different but with consistent overall similarities. Kathryn Connor and Jonathan Davidson developed their own framework for emotional resilience, creating a psychological testing instrument to measure this construct.[8] The Connor-Davidson Resilience Scale is one of the best validated and heavily researched instruments in the area of emotional resilience. Statistical analysis of this test has revealed distinct aspects of emotional resilience. Connor and Davidson described these factors as (1) a sense of personal competence and tenacity, (2) tolerance of negative affect and acceptance of the strengthening effects of stress, (3) acceptance of change and cultivating secure relationships, (4) a sense of control, and (5) spiritual influences.[9]

---

7 Linda S. Reeves, "Claim the Blessings of Your Covenants," *Ensign*, November 2013, 120.

8 Kathryn M. Connor and Jonathan R.T. Davidson, "Development of a New Resilience Scale: The Connor-Davidson Resilience Scale (CD-RISC)," *Depression and Anxiety*, September 2003, 76–82.

9 Salisu and Hashim, "A Critical Review of Scales Used in Resilience Research," 23–33.

Exploring these concepts from a scientific *and* spiritual perspective constitutes the bulk of this text. In addition, you will be invited to engage in exercises of thought and behavior to help develop these skills. The gospel of Jesus Christ is a gospel of action; improvement comes as we choose to engage and change for the better. The Savior taught that both hearing *and* living His teachings are what establish a sure foundation and keep us safe when storms of adversity beat upon us (see 3 Nephi 14:24–27). Hearing the truth gets us pointed in the right direction. *Living* the truth gets us moving toward healthy and heavenly destinations. Similarly, reading the concepts in this book will help you develop a greater understanding of truth. As you strive to apply these concepts to your own life, you can experience growth and progress.

Each chapter has a corresponding appendix with questions to consider, scriptures to ponder, and an invitation to create a personal plan of action. I have provided some direction, but the overall structure is minimal by design. I encourage you to review and complete the exercises in the appendices. Further, I invite you to prayerfully seek the guidance of the Holy Ghost in this process. He is the ultimate source of truth. He will help you develop personalized plans for growth that will be perfectly suited to your situation. Some of you may feel you are so weak that applying these concepts seems beyond reach. Take courage, for your Father in Heaven knows your weakness and will bless you with strength as you ask in faith. Just do your best and strive to be a little better each day.

Thought Journal

What are two or three things from this chapter that you'd like to remember?

Please see Appendix A for additional exercises for Chapter One.

CHAPTER TWO
THE BLESSINGS OF DISRUPTION

Trials originate from various sources. Sometimes they are the results of sin. A person who decides to rob a bank will be subject to any number of difficult consequences directly related to his decision to break the law. Other times, trials come from natural events. A recent windstorm wreaked havoc on our local area. Many trees were toppled. I saw a social media post in which a person's car was destroyed by a fallen tree. The person had done nothing wrong, yet still had to deal with the financial and temporal distress that ensued from their car being demolished. And then there are other times when the Lord introduces difficulty into our lives to help us learn valuable spiritual lessons. Some have a hard time understanding that the Lord might actually be the author of certain challenges, but in some cases it is true. Let me provide an example.

Alma the Elder was a priest of King Noah. From what we can tell, he behaved wickedly during that season of his life, openly disobeying the commandments of God. Abinadi bore powerful testimony before the king's court. We know most of the rebellious priests did not repent, continuing their immoral behavior and creating problems for others (see Mosiah 20). However, Alma the Elder had the opposite reaction. He believed the words of Abinadi and diligently sought to change his ways. He repented of his sinful past, preached the truths taught by Abinadi, and established a church. Many others followed his lead, and they became a righteous and blessed people. Then, without warning, a Lamanite army discovered their newly established city. Alma's people were forced into bondage, made to carry heavy burdens, and even forbidden to pray vocally. Why would such a thing happen to a righteous people? Mormon explains, "Nevertheless the Lord seeth fit to chasten his people; yea, he trieth their patience and their faith" (Mosiah 23:21). It was the *Lord* who chastened His people; it was *He* who tried their patience and faith. It wasn't some arbitrary life event or the random result of wicked behavior; the Lord knew this experience would be instructive and refining for Alma's people. And truly it was. The subsequent account of their redemption from bondage is a story of faith that has been inspiring for generations (see Mosiah 24).

Regardless of the sources of trials, the outcomes of trials all have the same potential possibilities. Perhaps the most significant prospective blessing is being able to grow closer to God and more fully recognize Him as the Source of our deliverance. Regarding Alma's people, Mormon commented,

> Whosoever putteth his trust in him the same shall be lifted up at the last day. Yea, and thus it was with this people. For behold, I will show unto you that they were brought into bondage, and none could deliver them but the Lord their God, yea, even the God of Abraham and Isaac and of Jacob. And it came to pass that he did deliver them, and he did show forth his mighty power unto them, and great were their rejoicings. (Mosiah 23:22–24)

Being brought into bondage created a situation in which the people had to depend upon the Lord. They humbly reached out for His help. The Lord exercised His power to deliver them, resulting in a greater bond between them and Him. Without this trial, Alma and his people would likely have continued to live righteous lives. But with this trial, they accelerated their spiritual growth and became better prepared to face future challenges. This seems to be one of the primary reasons the Lord either permits or introduces difficulty into our lives—so that we can become stronger and more resilient.

The late Clayton Christensen was a business scholar and faithful Latter-day Saint. One of his most significant ideological contributions was the idea of disruption, particularly in the business world. Brother Christensen developed the theory of "disruptive innovation," which is the process by which a small, unorthodox concept ends up creating significant change in an established business model. This leads the entire industry to experience growth that benefits society at large. It is the opposite of the old adage "If it ain't broke, don't fix it." Disruptive innovation basically says, "Let's take something that works fine, break it, and rebuild it even better than it was before." Consider this familiar example:

The advent of home video in the mid-1970s was a huge leap forward for home entertainment. Movies that were previously only available on the big screen could now be seen in the family room, anytime a person wanted, on their television. All it took was one of these new VCR gadgets, which quickly flew off the shelves and made their way to millions of households throughout the world. However, purchasing the movie cartridges could be expensive. And what if you didn't want to own the movie but just wanted to watch it once? There was no real solution to this until the late 1980s, when the first Blockbuster Video stores started to open. Although they had their competitors, they were easily the largest retail outlet of their kind. You could wander into your local Blockbuster (and there were plenty of them, over 9,000 stores worldwide at their peak), browse their selection of movies, and rent a copy for a few days at a fraction of the cost of purchasing the video outright. As DVDs came into being and gained popularity, the company pivoted and rented those as well. Blockbuster had filled a need and was a hugely successful company with no end in sight to their profits and success. And then, in the mid-2000s, some creative folks started to have other ideas.

With the advent of the internet, additional technologies became possible. Some people thought, *It's kind of a hassle to have to go to the movie store to rent a movie. And their selection can be a bit limited. What if people could rent movies online, from the convenience of their homes?* And thus Netflix was born, offering people the ability to rent movies via the internet and, in the early days of Netflix, receive them by mail. Their selection eventually eclipsed any local Blockbuster store, and customers could keep the movie longer and just drop it in their mailbox to return it. This new innovation probably worried the executives at Blockbuster.

Then another clever person thought, *Why do we need a brick-and-mortar store to rent a DVD from? What if we put them in vending machines and put those machines all over the place? And what if we could return DVDs to any machine, not just the one we rented it from?* And thus Redbox was born, offering extreme convenience that movie rental stores could not touch. If Blockbuster executives weren't worried by that point, they should have been.

The next ten years brought significant disruption to the movie-rental market, with brick-and-mortar stores slowly crumbling due to the convenience and selection of Netflix and Redbox. As home internet bandwidth increased, Netflix and other services began streaming movies and TV shows directly to home televisions. Streaming services are now ubiquitous, with hundreds of millions of subscribers worldwide. Redbox continues to offer rental services but is completely eclipsed by streaming services' offerings. And as of 2020, Blockbuster has only one store left open in the entire world. It took only about ten years for their massive operation to be decimated by a couple of small, strange ideas that took hold and sustained incredible growth. Netflix revolutionized the home movie market, with many other companies (e.g., Hulu, Amazon Prime Video, Disney+, VUDU) following their lead. One wonders what the next "small idea" will be that will disrupt the current market. Regardless of the tragedy this experience was for Blockbuster and its investors, Netflix and Redbox paved the way for an entirely new system that provides enhanced convenience, choice, and entertainment worldwide. Ultimately, good things came of such disruption.

Outside of the business world, disruption happens in our personal lives all the time. Deviations from well-laid plans seem to be a matter of course. An old Yiddish proverb states, "Man plans and God laughs." In other words, our Father in Heaven may be amused by the great confidence we place in our meager mortal perspective. It's not that we should sit around and wait for things to happen. On the contrary, we are commanded to be "anxiously engaged" in the planning of our lives (D&C 58:27). The difficulty arises when we create these plans on our own, without consulting the Spirit or using our Father's wisdom to inform our preparation. We are absolutely expected to fully use the moral agency we've been blessed with, but we are also to use that power in concert with heavenly consultation and humble deference to true inspiration. If we make plans without seeking our Heavenly Father's input, such plans are likely to be disrupted on a frequent basis. Even if we make plans with revelation and spiritual insight, our plans may still be disrupted on occasion, if only because disruption has such great potential to bring about needed change. One of the keys of emotional stability is to learn to embrace disruption as a tool for personal growth.

Consider the example of Adam and Eve in the Garden of Eden. Having no memory of their previous lives, all they knew were the blessings and comforts of the garden. Gorgeous flowers bloomed, delicious fruits abounded, and peace was the daily fare. It was a comfortable, serene existence. They had contact with their Father in Heaven and loved Him greatly. Despite their innocence, they knew He was different from them and admired Him for it. Day after day, their lives continued in happiness and harmony. Then things became disrupted. A charismatic stranger entered their world, tempting them to break one of the few commandments we know they had received. They had been prohibited from partaking of the fruit of the tree of knowledge of good and evil, being warned that if they did, they would die. In the Pearl of Great Price, we read how Satan tempted Eve, telling her she would *not* die if she partook of that fruit but that she and Adam would "be as gods" (Moses 4:11). This may have been particularly tempting given Adam and Eve's admiration of our Father in Heaven. After careful consideration of the consequences, Eve likely understood that the blessings of partaking of that fruit would be more significant than the price to be paid for the transgression. Adam partook as well. They gained knowledge from their actions but also experienced the consequences of exile from the garden and spiritual and physical separation from their Father in Heaven. Fortunately, Jesus Christ was ready to mend that breach and has done so through His magnificent Atonement and Resurrection.

To say that Adam and Eve's lives had been disrupted is an understatement. Going from the comforts of the garden to the complications of the world was an extremely stark transition. Opposition was now the daily fare, and Adam and Eve experienced pushback on everything from growing food to raising children. One might wonder if they ever looked back with regret on their decision to partake of the fruit. Did they make the right choice? Were there times when they looked fondly toward the Garden of Eden, thinking they had squandered a good thing? We don't have to wonder because scripture tells us exactly how they felt about their choice and subsequent expulsion:

> And in that day Adam blessed God and was filled, and began to prophesy concerning all the families of the earth, saying: Blessed be the name of God, for because of my transgression my eyes are opened, and in this life I shall have joy, and again in the flesh I shall see God.
>
> And Eve, his wife, heard all these things and was glad, saying: Were it not for our transgression we never should have had seed, and never should have known good and evil, and the joy of our redemption, and the eternal life which God giveth unto all the obedient.
>
> And Adam and Eve blessed the name of God, and they made all things known unto their sons and their daughters. (Moses 5:10–12)

It seems clear that Adam and Eve fully embraced the consequences of their choice, focusing on the advantages rather than the disadvantages. The disruption resulting from their decision led to greater happiness. It also provided significant growth opportunities. When Adam and Eve returned to their celestial home, they were not simply coming back the same as they were when they left. Through trial and difficulty, they acquired divine characteristics that made them like their Heavenly Parents. The same heavenly attributes they admired in the Garden of Eden became theirs through their diligent effort and the Savior's grace.

Seeing disruption as a tool for personal growth is critical in our spiritual and emotional development. Elder Neal A. Maxwell was diagnosed with leukemia *while serving* as a member of the Quorum of the Twelve Apostles. Talk about disruption! The schedules of these Brethren are demanding and relentless. They travel throughout the world to preach the gospel and witness of the resurrected Lord. In almost every case they are elderly and subject to the energy-draining effects of older age. Adding cancer and its associated treatments to the existing demands upon an Apostle would be beyond difficult. The story is told of how Elder Maxwell was considering why he had been afflicted with this dread disease at such a critical time in his life. As related by Brother M. Joseph Brough, former Second Counselor in the Young Men General Presidency, Elder Maxwell stated, "I was doing some pensive pondering and these 13 instructive and reassuring words came into my mind: 'I have given you leukemia that you might teach my people with authenticity.'"[10] Please take note; the Lord told Elder Maxwell that *He* (the Lord) had given him cancer, with a very specific purpose in mind. *He* had introduced this great disruption into Elder Maxwell's life, with the goal of helping him increase in efficacy as a teacher. Several years prior to his leukemia diagnosis, Elder Maxwell made the following statement in general conference:

> How could there be refining fires without enduring some heat? Or greater patience without enduring some instructive waiting? Or more empathy without bearing one another's burdens—not only that others' burdens may be lightened, but that we may be enlightened through greater empathy? How can there be later magnification without enduring some present deprivation?[11]

---

10 M. Joseph Brough, "Lift Up Your Head and Rejoice," *Ensign*, November 2018, 13.
11 Neal A. Maxwell, "Endure It Well," *Ensign*, April 1990, churchofjesuschrist.org/study/general-conference/1990/04/endure-it-well?lang=eng. Accessed October 20, 2020.

Disruptions can create opportunities for spiritual growth and progress. That path is almost always lined with adversity. In fact, it seems like this process is one of the more effective ways to become like our Savior.

To be clear, disruption does not *automatically* lead to increased emotional and spiritual growth. It simply creates a crossroads where we can choose how to proceed. Some choose the path of adversity and progression, while others choose easier paths that yield little change. Still others feel too weak to proceed, remaining stuck in their situation. Speaking about the relationship between disruption and emotional resilience, Connor and Davidson stated,

> In time, response to this disruption is a reintegrative process, leading to one of four outcomes: (1) the disruption represents an opportunity for growth and increased resilience, whereby adaptation to the disruption leads to a new, higher level of homeostasis; (2) a return to baseline homeostasis, in an effort to just get past or beyond the disruption; (3) recovery with loss, establishing a lower level of homeostasis; or (4) a dysfunctional state in which maladaptive strategies (e.g., self-destructive behaviors) are used to cope with stressors.[12]

Let's examine each of these potential reactions.

The first reaction is the most optimal; the individual not only endures the disruption but increases their overall capacity for stress. They become better and stronger because of their challenges. From there, the possible reactions to disruption get less and less helpful. In the second reaction, the individual is able to tolerate the disruption, hanging on without enduring any losses but also not making any gains. They end up right back where they started. The third reaction happens when the individual survives the adversity but ends up with greater problems than they had before. The fourth and worst outcome is when the individual develops new negative patterns of behavior that create ongoing distress. The last result is essentially the opposite of the first outcome.

To use an example, let's say a person experiences disruption by losing their employment. In the first reaction, the person might get additional training and education, engage in a serious search, and end up finding better employment than before. In the second reaction, the person may endure the

---

12 Connor and Davidson, "Development of a New Resilience Scale: The Connor-Davidson Resilience Scale (CD-RISC)," 77.

period of unemployment and then get hired back at their previous job or a similar one. In the third reaction, the person cannot find new employment and goes into debt. In the fourth reaction, the person can't find a new job, incurs significant personal debt, and descends into depression.

Clearly, we should strive for the first outcome as we deal with life's difficulties. I'm not suggesting all outcomes are within our control; they are not. There are many, many situations in which we have little influence over certain results. If a person loses a job, that doesn't mean that they will automatically be able to find amazing employment. Strong efforts often yield good results, but there are many other factors that can affect outcomes. However, just because the top tier might not always be within reach, that doesn't mean we should stop working for it. If we set our sights on a third- or fourth-place finish, we are not likely to achieve any more than that. We should strive for healthy outcomes and do our best to reach them. Sometimes all we can do is just hold on for a time, but we should yet endeavor to move forward when possible. When it comes to responding to disruption, we need to view this as a growth opportunity and apply our best efforts to sustain positive changes throughout the process.

Consider some examples from nature of how disruption leads to growth. A seed cannot become a plant unless it is broken down. Much-needed rain happens only when clouds break and release their moisture. Muscles need to be broken down in order to become stronger. It is through the breaking that progress occurs. This concept has been taught to disciples of Jesus Christ for millennia. After His death, Jesus taught the Nephites that He had fulfilled the law of Moses. Instead of offering animal sacrifices, they would offer a more personal, difficult sacrifice: "And ye shall offer for a sacrifice unto me a broken heart and a contrite spirit. And whoso cometh unto me with a broken heart and a contrite spirit, him will I baptize with fire and with the Holy Ghost" (3 Nephi 9:20). No one can make this sacrifice on our behalf, and no one can loan us the means to do so. Each of us has to choose to break our hearts, symbolically sacrificing our will to the Savior. We have to break our pride, our selfish ambition, our deviant habits, and our entertaining distractions. We have to put them on the altar and freely give them in exchange for something far better. Disruption helps with that breaking process. Sometimes it shakes us out of old routines and helps us see new options. Other times it creates forks in the road where we can choose new destinations. At any rate, it helps us reach the point where we can rebuild ourselves into something stronger and better and paves the way for greater emotional resilience.

Thought Journal

What are two or three things you'd like to remember from this chapter?

Please see Appendix B for additional exercises for Chapter Two.

CHAPTER THREE
UNDERSTANDING IDENTITY AND PURPOSE

People have always dealt with personal trials and difficulties, and a common one today is pornography. I've worked with several clients on this issue. Striving to increase my professional understanding, I've gained insights from books, articles, and professional conferences. But one day I heard a six-word phrase that provided more insight into managing pornography addiction than all I had previously learned. Elder Tad R. Callister, former member of the Quorum of the Seventy and former Sunday School General President, was in a training with President Russell M. Nelson in the early 2010s. One of the attendees asked the question, "How can we help those struggling with pornography?" Elder Callister recorded President Nelson's simple and profound response: "Teach them their identity and purpose."[13] Six words. Six words that better explain how to manage pornography addiction than I had ever heard before. Since then I have long pondered on President Nelson's wisdom regarding this issue. I have considered how it applies to many of life's struggles, not just problems with pornography. In 2018 Elder Brian K. Taylor expanded on President Nelson's counsel, stating that it could help with all personal challenges.[14] I was convinced and feel strongly that understanding our identity and purpose can help us effectively endure adversity. Indeed, developing a personal appreciation of this concept is foundational in creating stronger emotional resilience.

Understanding our identity and purpose originates in our thinking. Who are we? What are we here to accomplish? If you consider these questions,

---

13 Tad R. Callister, "Our Identity and Our Destiny," (Brigham Young University devotional, August 4, 2012), speeches.byu.edu/talks/tad-r-callister/our-identity-and-our-destiny/. Accessed October 22, 2020.
14 Brian K. Taylor, "Am I a Child of God?" *Ensign*, May 2018, 12.

you may have any number of thoughts. Some of the things we commonly associate with our identities include:

- Race and heritage (e.g., German, Chinese, African American, Latina)
- Career (e.g., plumber, lawyer, writer, teacher)
- Sexuality (e.g., straight, gay, lesbian)
- Hobbies (e.g., cyclist, runner, gardener)

Although our identities can be somewhat static, understanding our purpose often varies with our season of life. College students often feel their main purpose is to graduate and get a job. Employees can feel their main purpose is to remain employed and provide for themselves and others. I have a good friend who is currently running for political office; right now, his main purpose is doing what he can to get elected. Being aware of our purpose can provide us with direction and drive. Positive thoughts about who we are and what we are supposed to do often lead to feelings of hope and motivation.

What happens when a person does not have a good understanding of their identity and purpose? What if their thoughts include, *I have no idea who I am or whether I matter* or *My life is pointless*? You can probably already conclude what types of feelings result from such thinking. These include sadness, despair, anxiety, and hopelessness; such emotions are often associated with lack of direction. Without direction, we tend to flounder. When I was a youth, I went to a summer camp and learned how to sail. We trained in very small boats only big enough for two people. Each of us had a job. One was to control the sail using a rope called the mainsheet, and the other was to control the rudder. We had to work in concert to move in the desired direction. If the person controlling the sail did not position it properly to catch the wind, we wouldn't go anywhere. If the person controlling the rudder did not move it correctly, we'd move but go in the wrong direction. If both of us stopped doing our jobs, we'd just sit there or possibly be blown about or even be capsized. The Apostle Paul taught of the danger of having no direction: "That we henceforth be no more children, tossed to and fro, and carried about with every wind of doctrine, by the sleight of men, and cunning craftiness, whereby they lie in wait to deceive" (Ephesians 4:14). When we lack appreciation of our identity and purpose, we become like a boat with no rudder or sail, tossed about and directionless and never reaching an intended destination. That can be a depressing and ineffective way to live.

Each of us has an overarching identity and purpose. Both of these are divine. I believe this is what President Nelson was referring to when he taught that understanding these two concepts can help us manage not only pornography addiction but truly all other problems. His dear wife Sister Wendy Watson Nelson told the following to a worldwide gathering of youth:

> I believe if you could see yourself living with your Heavenly Parents and with Jesus Christ; if you could observe what you did premortally and see yourself making commitments—even covenants—with others, including your mentors and teachers; if you could see yourself courageously responding to attacks on truth and valiantly standing up for Jesus Christ, I believe that every one of you would have the increased power, increased commitment, and eternal perspective to help you overcome *any* and *all* of your confusion, doubts, struggles, and problems. *All* of them![15]

Understanding our true identities leads to discovering our divine purpose, which can inspire direction, motivation, and power. It's like having both people in a boat, working seamlessly together, heading confidently and quickly to the intended destination.

There are aspects of emotional resilience that relate to the concept of understanding identity and purpose as well. In a previous chapter we discussed the five factors of resilience as proposed by Connor and Davidson: (1) a sense of personal competence and tenacity, (2) tolerance of negative affect and acceptance of the strengthening effects of stress, (3) acceptance of change and cultivating secure relationships, (4) a sense of control, and (5) spiritual influences.[16] In a study of these factors, researchers Iacoviello and Charney concluded the following:

> Factors 1, 2, and 4 include cognitive components: patterns of thinking and core beliefs that, when confronted with stressful or traumatic situations, lead one to believe they can endure and

---

[15] Wendy W. Watson, "Hope of Israel" (worldwide devotional for young adults, June 3, 2018, churchofjesuschrist.org/study/broadcasts/worldwide-devotional-for-young-adults/2018/06/hope-of-israel?lang=eng. Accessed October 22, 2020.

[16] Connor and Davidson, "Development of a New Resilience Scale: The Connor-Davidson Resilience Scale (CD-RISC)," 76–82.

survive. Factors 1 and 3 include behavioral components: being active and engaged in one's response to stress or traumatic situations, and actively cultivating relationships and social support networks that will enable valuable resources when confronting and recovering from these situations.[17]

Note how Iacoviello and Charney's two-faceted summary of the five original factors lines up with the concepts of identity and purpose. Their first thought is that one of the core factors relates to "patterns of thinking and core beliefs." Understanding one's identity is most certainly a core belief, perhaps even the most fundamental of all core beliefs. What we believe about our character can come to color our entire lives. The researchers further explain how the second core factor of resilience relates to behavioral issues: "being active and engaged in one's response to stress or traumatic situations." This resonates with the concept of purpose or direction. Developing an appreciation of our identity gets us pointed in the right direction; understanding our purpose gets us moving. The combination of these two truths is a powerful tool to help us endure and grow from stressful situations.

One of Satan's more sophisticated deceptions is to confuse us as to our identity and purpose. To accomplish this, he often uses the tool of distraction. Our world has become increasingly more distracting, with new diversions available each minute. Mental and emotional discipline are required to stay focused on what is important. Not all distractions are bad, but they can keep us from moving forward if we are not careful. Steven W. Owen, former Young Men General President of The Church of Jesus Christ of Latter-day Saints, related this story:

> Not long ago I woke up and prepared to study the scriptures. I picked up my smartphone and sat in a chair next to my bed with the intention of opening the Gospel Library app. I unlocked my phone and was just about to begin studying when I saw a half dozen notifications for text messages and emails that had come during the night. I thought, "I'll quickly check those messages, and then I'll get right to the scriptures." Well, two hours later I was still reading text

---

[17] Brian M. Iacoviello and Dennis S. Charney, "Psychosocial Facets of Resilience: Implications for Preventing Posttrauma Psychopathology, Treating Trauma Survivors, and Enhancing Community Resilience," *European Journal of Psychotraumatology*, October 2014, 2.

messages, emails, news briefs, and social media posts. When I realized what time it was, I frantically rushed to get ready for the day. That morning I missed my scripture study, and consequently I didn't get the spiritual nourishment I was hoping for.[18]

In this example, Brother Owen was being responsible yet was still distracted from his primary purpose at that moment. He inadvertently sacrificed what was more important due to being distracted. The truth is there likely would have been ample time later that day for him to respond to texts, emails, and check important news stories. I have had similar experiences. While studying my scriptures a notification will often appear on my phone. Sometimes I have attended to the distraction rather than focusing on the task at hand. Distraction can happen almost subconsciously, often when we are not being intentional about our plans. I've noticed that if I have a clear direction for my day, I tend to be very productive and accomplish almost everything on my to-do list. But when I'm less intentional and less directed with my plans, I find I don't accomplish much at all. I'm not saying every step has to be scripted and planned in advance, but the more distraction we tolerate, the less likely we are to have a clear sense of identity and purpose.

As part of his prophetic preparation, Moses had a personal face-to-face interview with God. As part of this experience, the Lord showed Moses a small piece of His innumerable creations. Even though the vision was limited to our earth, Moses saw extensive creations and peoples, which caused him to "greatly marvel" (Moses 1:8). As God showed him these things, He spoke with Moses about his calling: "And *I have a work for thee*, Moses, *my son*" (Moses 1:6; emphases added). While details were not discussed at this time, God outlined the overarching principles of Moses's mission. Notice the two core features of the Lord's words: "And I have a work for thee, Moses, my son." Who was Moses? He was Heavenly Father's son. What was Moses's job? God had defined it for him as a work for him to accomplish. Moses's *identity* ("my son") and *purpose* ("a work") were established by the Lord. Moses had a mighty task to perform, one that would be fraught with stress, difficulty, and trauma. In preparation, God armed Moses with two powerful tools to help Moses endure. He taught Moses who he was and what he was about.

God's presence was upon him for their interview, enabling Moses to withstand the powerful glory of celestial beings. After the Lord departed, taking

---

18 Steven S. Owen, "Be Faithful, Not Faithless," *Ensign*, November 2019, 12.

His glory with Him, Moses collapsed and was unconscious for several hours. Upon awakening, he reflected on the things he had been shown and taught, perhaps considering his newly discovered divine identity and purpose. But his time of peaceful reflection was soon interrupted. Satan came to Moses, tempting him with lies and distorted truth. His initial words were succinct and devilishly deceptive: "Moses, son of man, worship me" (Moses 1:12). Let's analyze this statement and contrast it with the heavenly realities Moses previously learned. "Moses, *son of man*." Whereas God had told Moses he was His son, Satan told Moses he was a "son of man." A normal, inconsequential son of man. Sons and daughters of God have amazing potential and divine designs. They are foreordained to inherit all their Father has. Children of men are weak, insignificant, and unimportant. Satan's cleverly worded introduction was a direct assault on Moses's true identity.

Beyond that, Satan's attack was double-pronged, designed to inflict twice the damage. The second portion of his simple, sinister statement was an invitation: "worship me." Truly, this is at the heart of all Satan's temptations. His original rebellion in the premortal existence was an attempt to get the Father's glory without following the outlined path to obtain it. When the Savior faced Satan's temptations during His mortal ministry, the adversary's final and most revealing temptation was to demand the Lord worship him. Satan is as power-hungry as they come, infinitely unsatisfied, and wants nothing more than to be the object of our collective worship. So it comes as no surprise that he would demand Moses's adoration and obedience. Consider how Moses's divinely appointed task would have been affected had Moses yielded to Satan's temptation. The Lord had "a work" for Moses. Surely this work did not involve worshiping His enemy. Satan sought to derail Moses's heavenly commission, attacking not only his identity but his purpose as well. So many of Satan's temptations and strategies are firmly targeted at those two foundational principles. If he can get these critical elements of our spiritual base to crumble, there is little left to keep us standing when the winds of adversity blow.

Instead of yielding to Satan's temptation, Moses relied on his renewed understanding of identity and purpose to muster strength. "And it came to pass that Moses looked upon Satan and said: Who art thou? For behold, I am a son of God, in the similitude of his Only Begotten; and where is thy glory, that I should worship thee?" (Moses 1:13) In other words, Moses said, "You aren't anything like my Father, but I am. I have a physical body that is created in His image. I know who I am. I am not going to worship you." Moses was not derailed from his path, as he possessed a clear understanding of who he was. Having an appreciation of our divine heritage gives meaning to life. It helps us be confident in our decisions and have a sense of belonging. We are all part of the glorious family of God, heirs to all He has.

As family history research has increased in popularity, people often want to know if they are related to royalty or other individuals considered by the world to be significant. Members of The Church of Jesus Christ of Latter-day Saints are impressed when they meet someone who is descended from Joseph or Hyrum Smith. While that can be impressive, we are all only one degree of separation from the most extraordinary being we will ever know. We are literal spirit children of exalted Heavenly Parents, who love us immensely. It's the most amazing pedigree ever and applies to all of us.

Moses continued to resist Satan's lure, stating, "I will not cease to call upon God, *I have other things to inquire of him*: for his glory has been upon me, wherefore I can judge between him and thee. Depart hence, Satan" (Moses 1:18; emphasis added). Moses had "other things to inquire," and he had more to do. God had told him He had a work for him, and Moses was eager to discover what that was and how he could get started. He didn't have time for Satan's distractions because he had a purpose and goal. When we have a clouded or distracted view of our purpose, it is much easier to deviate from a productive course. If one believes they have no purpose at all, then there can be very little motivation to progress. Not only did Moses have a purpose, but *we each have a purpose as well*. We can discover our specific purposes the same way Moses did, by inquiring of God. Patriarchal blessings are wonderful tools to help us understand the very unique work Father in Heaven would like us to accomplish in life. Continuing revelation can help us learn, line upon line, about our role in the ongoing Restoration of the gospel of Jesus Christ. Moses rebuffed Satan's temptation and used the core concepts of his identity and purpose to strengthen his resolve.

However, Satan did not give up that easily. In a rare insight into his rage, the scriptures record, "And now, when Moses had said these words, Satan cried with a loud voice, and ranted upon the earth, and commanded, saying: I am the Only Begotten, worship me" (Moses 1:19). This reaction terrified Moses, and his determination started to wobble. Knowing that his strength alone would be insufficient to withstand Satan, Moses pleaded for help: "Nevertheless, calling upon God, *he received strength*, and he commanded, saying: Depart from me, Satan, for this one God only will I worship, which is the God of glory" (Moses 1:20; emphasis added). Reemphasizing his divine purpose ("this one God only will I worship"), Moses got additional spiritual strength to resist the adversary. His mortal resolve, combined with the marvelous powers of heaven, was sufficient to drive Satan out. This pattern is instructive to us as well. Having a good understanding of our identity and purpose will surely help us endure trials and repel temptations. However, our efforts alone will almost always be lacking. Like Moses, we need the sustaining and strengthening effect of the Holy Ghost to ultimately triumph over our enemy.

Jean B. Bingham, Relief Society General President, stated:

> Because of the power He gives us as we are obedient, we are able to become more than we ever could on our own. We may not understand completely how, but each of us who has felt faith in Christ increase has also received a greater understanding of our divine identity and purpose, leading us to make choices that are consistent with that knowledge.[19]

As trials continue and pressures mount, it can be difficult to maintain strength equal to our challenges. This teaching suggests that those who have a clear sense of direction, with a belief that their path is consistent with Heavenly Father's desires, can develop greater emotional and spiritual resolve to continue in the face of difficulty. Understanding our divine identity and eternal purpose will increase our capacity for emotional resilience.

THOUGHT JOURNAL

What are two or three things you'd like to remember from this chapter?

Please see Appendix C for additional exercises for Chapter Three.

---

19 Jean B. Bingham, "That Your Joy Might Be Full," *Ensign*, November 2017, 86.

CHAPTER FOUR
THE SAVIOR'S ENABLING POWER

WHILE IN HIGH SCHOOL, I considered various ideas for my future career. My father was an engineer and encouraged me to pursue training in the hard sciences, yet I found I had a knack for understanding people, so my thoughts turned to the social sciences. Originally, I wanted to be a child psychiatrist, which would require a medical school education. Ultimately, I decided to become a psychologist, with the goal to be a university professor. While receiving my undergraduate education at Brigham Young University, I developed a strong affection for the program and school. I felt like BYU would be the best place for me to work as a professor, and I started planning for this. I intended to seek graduate education somewhere other than BYU, diversifying my knowledge and increasing my chances of eventually getting hired at BYU, but I ended up earning my bachelor's, master's, and doctoral degrees all from BYU, despite attempts to get admitted to other universities. With my less-than-diverse educational experience, I wondered how I would fulfill my dream of being a BYU professor.

In time, it became clear the Lord had very different plans for my career. Decades later, I look back and realize I was never intended to be a BYU professor. I was to become a psychologist in private practice and, ultimately, an author and public speaker. I was to help thousands upon thousands of individuals with their mental health issues. Above all, I was to learn how the principles of the restored gospel can help people improve their mental and emotional health. What I didn't realize before was that receiving all my education at BYU was excellent preparation to increase my understanding of how the gospel and mental health interact. I was able to sift through the multitude of psychological interventions I learned and adopt those principles that were in harmony with the gospel while avoiding practices that were inconsistent with revealed truth. In retrospect, I am profoundly grateful for my career path and how the Lord directed me in ways I could not see from the outset.

With an increased understanding of how the principles of the gospel of Jesus Christ can help manage mental health issues, I routinely suggest prayer, scripture study, going to church, temple attendance, and other essential spiritual practices as beneficial to improving mental health. When I make such recommendations, some express the following concern: "You can't just pray away mental health issues." I completely agree. Frankly, I don't think we can "pray away" any of our trials, but that doesn't mean prayer is unnecessary to the process. Most of the time, when we pray for assistance, we receive direction about what *we* need to do in order to solve the problem. Consider the example of the prophet Nephi, when his father's family arrived on the shores of Bountiful. They were ecstatic to be out of the desert, at a beautiful beach that was teeming with food. Yet Bountiful was not their final destination. They needed to cross the ocean to arrive at the promised land. The Lord commanded Nephi to go into the mountain, where He gave him the following instruction: "Thou shalt construct a ship, after the manner which I shall show thee, that I may carry thy people across these waters" (1 Nephi 17:8).

Notice the division of responsibility in this statement. Nephi had a job to do; he was to construct a ship. The Lord had a job to do; He would carry Lehi's family across the waters. The Lord was able to complete His portion of the task without Nephi's involvement—there are multiple examples in scripture of when prophets were transported from place to place by the Spirit. The Lord could have simply relocated Lehi's family from Bountiful to America in an instant. For that matter, He could have taken them from Jerusalem to America in the same fashion, avoiding the drama of their going back for the brass plates, Nephi breaking his bow, Sariah mourning what she thought was the death of her sons, and dozens of other grievous trials. If arriving at the ultimate destination were the only goal, then heavenly transportation may have been the best option. But that was not the only goal. Lehi and company were to arrive in the promised land *after* having endured hardships, providing them the chance to develop greater faith and trust in God. I am confident the journey from Jerusalem to America was a significant and formative spiritual experience for Lehi's faithful posterity.

It is true that you can't just "pray away" mental health issues, or any personal trial for that matter. You also can't just "fast away" or "church away" or "temple away" such issues either. But as we seek the Lord's help with our difficulties, He reveals ways for us to help ourselves. In Nephi's case, He showed him how to build a boat. Nephi and his family members had to do all the building, but the Lord showed them how. In the case of dealing with mental health challenges, perhaps prayer and other spiritual practices lead to revelation about a counselor to talk with or a medication to take or a behavioral pattern to change. The Lord is the architect who designs the remedies; we are the workers who implement the process. In His wisdom, our Heavenly Father requires action on our part. This not only helps us righteously exercise our moral agency but also helps us develop celestial characteristics that sanctify our souls. This growing and cleansing process is made possible through the Savior's Atonement.

To my understanding, the Atonement of Jesus Christ serves three primary purposes. First, it rescues us from physical death. When Adam and Eve were expelled from the Garden of Eden, they also became mortal, subject to physical death. That same condition was imposed on all their posterity. Death would have ended our eternal progression, for without our physical bodies, we could not become like our Father in Heaven. The Savior's Resurrection broke the bands of death and provided a universal rescue for all of Father's children who enter into mortality. "For as in Adam all die, even so in Christ shall all be made alive" (1 Corinthians 15:22).

Second, the Savior's Atonement provides potential rescue from the effects of sin. Upon reaching the age of accountability, we become responsible for our own sinful choices. Because no "unclean thing [can] enter into the kingdom of God" (1 Nephi 15:34), our sins would forever keep us from returning to our Father's presence, but since Jesus Christ paid the debt of sin owed by all mankind, we can receive forgiveness upon the condition of repentance. While this is not a free gift like resurrection, it is available to all who humble themselves and sincerely seek the Savior's mercy.

I find that these first two purposes of the Savior's Atonement are widely understood among members of The Church of Jesus Christ of Latter-day Saints. However, the third purpose is not as readily appreciated. I speak of the enabling power of the Atonement of Jesus Christ. It is aptly described by Alma the Younger, as he taught the saints in Gideon:

> And he shall go forth, suffering pains and afflictions and temptations of every kind; and this that the word might be fulfilled which saith *he will take upon him the pains and the sicknesses of his people.* And he will take upon him death, that he may loose the bands of death which bind his people; *and he*

> *will take upon him their infirmities, that his bowels may be filled with mercy, according to the flesh, that he may know according to the flesh how to succor his people according to their infirmities.* (Alma 7:11–12; emphases added)

Concerning the Savior's Atonement, His Resurrection takes care of physical death, and His suffering for our sins takes care of spiritual death. So why did He have to feel our pains, sicknesses, and infirmities on top of the crushing weight of everyone's sins? Alma explains why; it's so the Savior would be "filled with mercy," knowing how to help us "according to the flesh." I think that means Jesus Christ wanted to experience the challenges we'd go through so He could truly understand us in our moments of difficulty. No mortal will ever be able to say, "Lord, you just don't know how hard it was." He knows *exactly* how difficult life is because He experienced it. *All* of it. For us.

What does the enabling power of the Atonement of Jesus Christ have to do with developing greater emotional resilience? It relates to our collective goal of becoming more like the Savior, increasing in spiritual and emotional strength, and how we achieve that objective. We were never intended to make this journey alone or solely with our own efforts. While our participation is critical, it is inadequate by itself. We need to rely on the strength the Savior can provide, through His enabling power, in order to make needed changes. Michelle D. Craig, First Counselor in the Young Women General Presidency, taught this point:

> Of course, all of us will fall short of our divine potential, and there is some truth in the realization that *alone* we are not enough. But the good news of the gospel is that with the grace of God, we *are* enough. With Christ's help, we can do all things.[20]

She notes how our limited understanding of the Atonement of Jesus Christ can contribute to the mistaken notion that somehow, we are expected to do everything on our own. This is not true. Not only are we not strong enough on our own but it is a true blessing to navigate life with the powerful help of our beloved Savior.

When Moroni was abridging the book of Ether, he commented on his own shortcomings. He was afraid that, due to his poor writing skills, future

---

20 Michelle D. Craig, "Divine Discontent," *Ensign*, November 2018, 54.

generations would mock his account. The Lord promised him that any weakness on his part would be made strong such that no one would fault him for his deficiencies. The Lord went on to tell Moroni,

> And if men come unto me I will show unto them their weakness. I give unto men weakness that they may be humble; and my grace is sufficient for all men that humble themselves before me; for if they humble themselves before me, and have faith in me, then will I make weak things become strong unto them. (Ether 12:27)

I find it interesting that when we are finally humble enough to go to the Lord, one of the first things He does is "show us" our weakness. It's like He doesn't want us to forget that we desperately need Him in order to move forward. This scriptural recipe for strength is clear: we humble ourselves, we have faith in Jesus Christ, and then He compensates for our weakness and makes us strong. It says nothing about developing strength exclusively on our own but in a partnership with the Lord. Our efforts are absolutely necessary, but the ultimate result will be a combination of our work and the Savior's grace. Sheri L. Dew, former Second Counselor in the Relief Society General Presidency, instructed:

> Our responsibility is to learn to draw upon the power of the Atonement. Otherwise we walk through mortality relying solely on our own strength. And to do that is to invite the frustration of failure and to refuse the most resplendent gift in time or eternity.[21]

Sometimes we wish the Lord would simply take away our trials, clearing the road before us so our path is smooth and easy. Knowing the deep love and compassion our Father in Heaven has for us, I have to believe there is a part of Him that wishes He could do just that. But because He is eternally wise, He knows challenges are an essential part of our development. Instead of removing the challenges, He offers us a portion of His strength so we can endure and succeed. When Alma the Younger and his missionary cohorts went to reclaim the apostate Zoramites, they were shocked at the doctrinal

---

21 Sheri L. Dew, "Our Only Chance," *Ensign*, May 1999, churchofjesuschrist.org/study/ensign/1999/05/our-only-chance?lang=eng. Accessed November 5, 2020.

deviations that had occurred. In general, the people were proud, wicked, and insensitive yet fully convinced they were in God's good graces (see Alma 31:8–23). Alma knew the task before them was difficult. In an eloquent prayer, he stated,

> O Lord God, how long wilt thou suffer that such wickedness and infidelity shall be among this people? O Lord, *wilt thou give me strength, that I may bear with mine infirmities.* For I am infirm, and such wickedness among this people doth pain my soul. O Lord, my heart is exceedingly sorrowful; wilt thou comfort my soul in Christ. O Lord, *wilt thou grant unto me that I may have strength, that I may suffer with patience these afflictions which shall come upon me,* because of the iniquity of this people. (Alma 31:30–31; emphases added)

Note what Alma actually prayed for and what he could have prayed for. He had infirmities that weakened him and complicated his journey. Did he pray for the Lord to remove his infirmities? No. He prayed for strength to bear with them. He knew his missionary service would cause him affliction. Did he pray for the affliction to be erased? For the Lord to clear his path? No. He prayed for the strength to suffer his afflictions with patience. This is a remarkable example for each of us. We have to experience difficulty; it is part of the plan of salvation. Opposition is essential in order for us to prove our faithfulness (see 2 Nephi 2:11). If the Lord removed the opposition, it would short-circuit His eternal designs. But in His loving, merciful way, He lets us lean on His arm as we walk the arduous roads that lead back to Him. He asks us to do our part, using as much strength as we can muster, and then provides additional help so the task is not overwhelming. I am overcome with gratitude and love for our Savior, whose magnanimous compassion is truly amazing.

Alma's prayer also reveals another critical principle for effective personal development. He prayed for strength to endure, not for the trials to be removed. By doing so, Alma cast himself as an actor in the process, as opposed to an observer. He wanted to remain involved in his own progress, doing the work for himself with the added support of the Lord. This gave him the chance to exercise agency and grow spiritually. If the Lord had simply removed the trial, then Alma would have been a mere observer.

I remember living in Wyoming when I was a child. My dad wanted a nice blanket of grass in our front yard, but the soil was filled with rocks, so he used a rototiller to turn up the soil and unearth the rocks, which we then put in a wheelbarrow and hauled out of the yard. Even though I was young, I was asked to participate to the best of my ability. To this day I can recall seeing the huge pile of rocks that we extracted from our yard. My dad taught me to work hard by *involving me in the process*, which has blessed my life for decades. Being an *actor* in the rock removal taught me critical life lessons and helped me develop patterns of endurance and industry. If I had simply been an *observer* in that process, perhaps I would have watched my dad from the window while sipping lemonade. I could still tell the tale of the front-yard transformation but would not have achieved the skills that came from acting. This is a critical point to understand: *we must be actors in our lives*. We must take responsibility and move forward to the best of our ability. Of course, we need to rely on the enabling power of the Savior's Atonement as we do this, but our participation is essential. Please do not forget this lesson; understanding and implementing it is one of the most crucial elements of our eternal progression.

Often, I hear people lament that they cannot change certain negative personality characteristics, claiming, "That's just the way I am." This is a dangerous deception. Satan would love to have us believe that we cannot change. This belief casts us as observers, instead of actors, in our life story. If you believe you cannot change something, then your efforts to change will likely be less motivated than they otherwise could be. Sometimes people have very ingrained behaviors, even those that might be influenced by brain chemistry, and feel helpless to do anything about it. Usually, such feelings of helplessness come from repeated attempts to change while experiencing only limited progress. It is very important to remember that some trials persist despite our best efforts. That does not mean we should stop trying. Trying to move forward, no matter how frustrating or seemingly unfruitful, will yield benefits. We will learn patterns of persistence and diligence. We will develop skills to cope with frustration and discouragement. What can seem like zero progress is actually an incremental process of developing heavenly characteristics that will benefit us in this life and the life to come. This is one of the reasons Satan wants us to believe we cannot change and therefore might as well cease our efforts to do so. He is opposed to any strategy that will help us become more like our Father in Heaven.

The prophet Mormon was called to lead a terrible, wicked people. They did not heed his words. They had doomed themselves to utter destruction, and Mormon was destined to helplessly witness it. At one point he wrote to his son Moroni regarding his difficult task. He related how, if he was bold with his followers, they got angry. If he tried a softer approach, they wouldn't listen. He couldn't win. Conventional wisdom would suggest one should stop trying at that point, as it was clearly a losing battle. But the Lord's work is usually anything but conventional. Mormon told Moroni,

> And now, my beloved son, notwithstanding their hardness, let us labor diligently; for if we should cease to labor, we should be brought under condemnation; for we have a labor to perform whilst in this tabernacle of clay, that we may conquer the enemy of all righteousness, and rest our souls in the kingdom of God. (Moroni 9:6)

Mormon's task was to call the people to repentance, not to *get* them to repent. He was able to accomplish his goal. He labored all his days, and although the people never heeded his words, he fulfilled his divine responsibility. This is another critical concept to understand. We need to work, every day, to make ourselves better. Whether that yields immediate results (think Ammon and his multitude of converts after only a few days in the mission field) or no changes whatsoever (think Mormon and his people being completely destroyed), *we need to work*. If Mormon had ceased to do his duty, he would have been cast as an observer, not an actor, in the process. When it comes to issues of personal change, our responsibility is to work every day, regardless of how much fruit that yields. I know some of you feel so weak that even the smallest effort seems monumental. I encourage you to try to do something every day, no matter how small, to move forward. I truly believe the greater blessing comes from the journey and the effort rather than arriving at the desired destination. As you attempt to implement the principles in this book, you will probably find some concepts easier to employ than others. Please try to avoid discouragement if progress seems slow. As long as you are trying every day to make needed changes, you are making more progress than you think.

We've previously discussed the essential nature of emotional resilience in managing life's trials. We cannot force trials to cease. They come to the obedient and disobedient alike. Our best hope is to develop the skills to effectively endure, and even grow from, the difficulties we face. This book is designed to help you obtain such skills. But if you approach this process alone, without seeking heavenly help, you will experience limited progress. We need the Lord's strength to amplify our abilities. As you consider the changes you can make in order to become more emotionally resilient, regularly seek the Savior's support and ask for strength to endure more effectively and improve over time.

THOUGHT JOURNAL

What are two or three things you'd like to remember from this chapter?

Please see Appendix D for additional exercises for Chapter Four.

CHAPTER FIVE
EMOTIONAL RESILIENCE ELEMENT #1: PERSONAL COMPETENCE

THE CONCEPT OF PERSONAL COMPETENCE has been widely discussed and often cited as an element of emotional intelligence. For the purposes of this book, we will define personal competence as the belief in one's ability to set and achieve goals. It is also related to the idea of self-confidence, meaning the degree to which one has assurance in her or his own capacities. Being able to endure difficulty has much to do with conviction in our own abilities to rise above trials. If we believe we are able to conquer, we have a much greater likelihood of positive outcomes than if we believe we are going to fail.

Martin Seligman is a psychologist who pioneered the concept of "learned helplessness."[22] Long before ethical research boards would have condemned such an experiment, Seligman investigated a dog's ability to learn to avoid punishment. He took one set of dogs, placed them in a cage, and administered a light electric shock. If the dog pressed a certain panel in the cage, the shock would end. Most dogs swiftly learned that pressing the panel relieved their distress. Then Seligman altered the scenario for a second set of dogs. He restrained the dogs so they could not press the panel, leaving them no way to avoid the shock. Whereas the first dogs learned they could end the distress by doing something, the second dogs learned that no matter what they did, the pain continued.

Seligman conducted a second phase of the experiment, this time placing the dogs in a shuttle box. This was a closed box with two sections, having a small but passable barrier in between. The floor of the box was rigged to administer a mild electric shock. He began with the first group of dogs, those who had learned to stop the electricity by pressing the panel. These dogs

---

22 Courtney E. Ackerman, "Learned Helplessness: Seligman's Theory of Depression (+ Cure)," Positive Psychology, April 3, 2021, positivepsychology.com/learned-helplessness-seligman-theory-depression-cure/

started on one side of the box, and the researcher activated the electricity on that side. As the dogs struggled to find a way to escape the shock (there were no panels to press this time), eventually they jumped over the barrier and found the other side was not electrified. Quickly, these dogs learned that once the shock was initiated, all they had to do was hop to the other side to avoid the jolt.

The second group of dogs was then tested. They had the same setup in the box but had previously learned that no matter what they did, they couldn't stop the shock. When the electricity was engaged for the second group of dogs, the dogs didn't do anything. Unlike their counterparts, they didn't search for a way to escape. They simply lay there and endured the shock. This is a heartbreaking scenario, which fortunately would never be permitted in contemporary psychological experimentation, but it revealed valuable information regarding the idea of personal competence. These dogs had the ability to alter their circumstance. What they lacked was the *belief* that they could alter their circumstance.

If you believe your car won't start, you probably won't turn the key. If you believe you won't get accepted to college, you might not apply. Perhaps the car runs fine and your prospects for college admission are good, but if you don't act, those outcomes are forever unknown. Having sufficient confidence and belief in oneself is essential to achieving goals and rising above tribulation. If you are faced with a daunting task but believe you cannot succeed, chances are you will be hesitant to even try. Such situations result in greater distress and increased lack of confidence. But the truth is you are more competent that you realize; you just need to come to believe this for yourself.

After fleeing Jerusalem with his family, Lehi received revelation that his sons were to return to obtain the plates of brass from Laban. This involved a days-long journey to meet with a man who had little interest in parting with the plates. Nephi and his brothers cast lots to determine who would ask Laban for the plates; the lot fell upon Laman. Laman visited with Laban and requested the plates. Laban reacted with anger, first accusing Laman of being a thief and then threatening to kill him. Laman barely escaped with his life, returning to his brothers to tell the harrowing tale. Laman and Lemuel were immediately ready to give up, but Nephi encouraged them that together they could fulfill their task. They came up with a second plan: they'd retrieve their abandoned riches from their home and use them to bribe Laban to part with the plates. This design failed as well. When Laban saw their wealth, he was duly impressed and simply stole it from them, having his guards chase Nephi and company from Laban's home. As the brothers fled and escaped to the safety of the cavity of a rock, Laman and Lemuel beat Nephi with a stick, only to be rebuked by an angel. The angel commanded them to return to Jerusalem to obtain the plates, stating the Lord would provide a way (see 1 Nephi 3).

The angelic presence had barely departed when Laman and Lemuel complained anew, stating, "How is it possible that the Lord will deliver Laban into our hands? Behold, he is a mighty man, and he can command fifty, yea, even he can slay fifty; then why not us?" (1 Nephi 3:31). Let's consider that statement in terms of personal competence, which is the belief in one's ability to set and achieve goals. Laman and Lemuel's level of personal competence, at least when it came to this situation, was low. They did not believe they could accomplish the task. They felt Laban was too powerful and too resourceful. This man could slay as many as fifty people; what chance did their small group have against such a formidable foe? Contrasted with Laman and Lemuel, Nephi responded with faith:

> And it came to pass that I spake unto my brethren, saying: Let us go up again unto Jerusalem, and let us be faithful in keeping the commandments of the Lord; for behold he is mightier than all the earth, then why not mightier than Laban and his fifty, yea, or even than his tens of thousands? (1 Nephi 4:1)

Nephi reminded them of the children of Israel and the Red Sea; if the Lord could literally open a sea and destroy an army, how could He not manage Laban and help their cause? Many are familiar with the story's conclusion: Nephi was successful in retrieving the plates with the Lord's assistance (see 1 Nephi 4).

In this circumstance of retrieving the brass plates, Nephi, Laman, and Lemuel all faced the same trial, yet their responses were dramatically different. Whereas Nephi believed he could succeed, Laman and Lemuel were convinced they would fail. While Nephi persisted until he accomplished the task, Laman and Lemuel were ready to give up after their first attempt. Nephi's confidence was key in helping him endure the difficulties he faced, which included losing his wealth, being beaten, and facing the fears of going back to a man who was clearly ready to kill him. One could say Nephi had a strong sense of personal competence; he believed in his ability to achieve the goal he had established. But his sense of competence was derived from more than just a healthy self-confidence or history of success. From a gospel perspective, we gain confidence as we develop faith in the Lord. How could Nephi have assurance he would succeed? All signs pointed to another failure, but he had faith that he could not fail in a divinely appointed task as long as he did his part. Remember his response to his father upon receiving the assignment: "I will go and do the things which the Lord hath commanded, for I know that the Lord giveth no commandments unto the children of men, save he shall prepare a way for them that they may accomplish the thing which he commandeth them" (1 Nephi 3:7). Nephi's sense of personal competence—his belief that he would meet his goal—was bolstered by his faith that God would support him in righteous endeavors. We can do the same. As we seek to increase our confidence to succeed, enlarging our faith in the Savior is critical.

Alma taught regarding faith, "And now as I said concerning faith—faith is not to have a perfect knowledge of things; therefore if ye have faith ye hope for things which are not seen, which are true" (Alma 32:21). Sometimes we say that faith is the first principle of the gospel; that's only partially correct. The first principle of the gospel is "faith *in the Lord Jesus Christ*" (Articles of Faith 1:4; emphasis added). We can have faith in any number of things: family members, friends, business strategies, and so on. But the foundational principle of the restored gospel of Jesus Christ is to have faith in Him. It means to trust Him. It means to accept His teachings and the teachings of His servants even when we don't fully understand. It means to take steps into the dark unknown, believing He will eventually light the way. Having faith in Jesus Christ is a companion principle to personal competence. When goals seem impossible, we are likely to retreat or give up in frustration. As we add faith in Jesus Christ to the equation, we can gain additional confidence that we will ultimately prevail.

An important element of this process is ensuring that our goals are *righteous* goals. We will not be divinely supported in ambitions that are contrary to the Father's will. Korihor, an anti-Christ, was quite successful in his goals. He sought to deceive people and obtain a large following and did precisely that. His preaching encouraged the saints to abandon their covenants and seek worldly pleasures. One could say that Korihor had a strong sense of personal competence. He set a goal and actively worked toward it, confident in his ultimate success. Yet his demise was ultimately unavoidable, as are those of all individuals or organizations who fight against the Lamb. Korihor's life ended in abject ruin, the completely opposite outcome from his lofty objectives. Mormon commented on the pathetic end of this detractor: "And thus we see the end of him who perverteth the ways of the Lord; and thus we see that the devil will not support his children at the last day, but doth speedily drag them down to hell" (Alma 30:60). Korihor's goal to destroy the Church was unrighteous and contrary to the Savior's purposes. In order to progress spiritually, we should set righteous goals. What constitutes a "righteous goal"? You'll have to answer that for yourself, in consultation with heaven. Personally, I think that any goal that promotes the overall mission of The Church of Jesus Christ of Latter-day Saints and is "virtuous, lovely, or of good report or praiseworthy" (Articles of Faith 1:13) is righteous. But that determination is up to each individual to discover. The Lord will help you identify and attain worthy objectives.

Let's talk about some common roadblocks that can get in the way of personal competence, or our ability to set and achieve goals:

Roadblock #1: Misunderstanding Our Purpose

Sometimes we have difficulty even setting goals because we don't truly understand the purpose of mortality. Some view their lives as something to merely be endured; they have to grit their teeth for eight or nine decades and just hold on until they are called back to their heavenly home. That is a mistaken notion that can lead to few joyful opportunities. Think about the parable of the talents; two of the servants improved their talents through risk and hard work. They probably set goals of how to increase their resources, then acted to implement their plans. Both servants received a fine reward, yet the third servant was afraid. Not wanting to lose what he had been given, he simply hid the talent he'd been given and awaited the Lord's return. His actions were ill-advised, and his fate was less than desirable (see Matthew 25:14–30). Mortality is designed for our growth and improvement, which involves setting goals and working to accomplish them. Understanding our purpose can help us find direction, which can naturally lead to setting and achieving goals.

Roadblock #2: Procrastination

Procrastination is an insidious roadblock. In such cases, we already have a goal; we just haven't gotten around to completing it yet. Sometimes we justify our lack of progress by stating that at least we have a goal, which is better than nothing. But there is truly no practical difference between remaining static with a goal in mind or remaining static with *no* goal in mind. In each case, there is stagnation. Procrastination can be borne of fear, laziness, feeling overwhelmed, or other circumstances that lead us to believe that it's better to stay still than to move forward. I wish I had an elegant solution to procrastination, but I don't. In decades of practicing psychology, I've found the best antidote for procrastination is to start working toward the goal. Breaking the task into smaller chunks can help, making it easier to get going. But the only real solution to being stuck is to get moving.

Roadblock #3: Lack of Sustained Effort

Setting goals can be the easy part; achieving goals is more challenging. Some goals, particularly difficult ones, are only achieved with consistent effort over time. Losing weight is a common goal for many. Perhaps the most tried and true method to losing weight is to exercise more and eat healthier. Let's consider this scenario: I set a goal to lose ten pounds. I weigh myself. I eat a healthy salad (good eating) and do ten pushups (exercise). Twenty minutes later I weigh myself again. I probably won't notice any decrease in my weight, considering the last time I weighed myself was only twenty minutes prior. So are healthy eating and exercise not effective? They *are* effective, but I haven't engaged long enough to see results. Sometimes we accuse the process as unsuccessful when the true culprit is a lack of ongoing effort. Depending on the goal, you might not see significant progress until you have worked at it for months or even years. Don't abandon goals prematurely; make sure you 1) are using a good strategy and 2) employ that strategy long enough to yield results. Remember, consistency is critical in this process. Even if you have only enough energy to move forward a little each day, that is preferable to no progress at all.

Chapter Five Exercise

Here is an opportunity for you to examine something specific in your life and determine possible approaches to increase your skill of personal competence.

Think of a goal you'd like to accomplish but that you either find difficult to set or move toward.

- What is the goal?

- Why do you want to meet this goal?

- What are the barriers to your completing the goal?

Now it's time for action. The following questions will help you create the start of a plan. You'll need to do additional work to form a complete strategy and may need help from others in doing so, but this will help get you moving.

- Break down your goal into smaller steps. What is one step toward your goal that you'd like to achieve within the next month?

- What is something you can do on a regular basis to take that step or work toward that goal?

- What is something you can do *today* to make progress on your goal?

Successfully achieving goals is usually based on long-term endurance rather than intense short-term effort. Consider the example of financial security. The stock market appeals to many due to its potential for significant returns on small investments. However, it can also be very volatile, with fortunes being wiped out in the course of a single day. Contrast that with a simple savings account, where money is consistently deposited. If you put $1,000 into a savings account when you are twenty years of age and consistently add $100 a month, even with a small interest rate, you would have over $100,000 in fifty years. I'm not suggesting specific financial investment strategies but am simply using this example to illustrate the power of small, sustained effort over time. You don't have to be super strong to meet your goals; you just have to be consistent.

Developing a better understanding of our purpose in mortality can be very helpful in increasing our motivation to set and achieve goals. In the premortal existence, we loved and revered our Father in Heaven. We had spirit bodies, but He has a glorified, resurrected body and possesses amazing personal characteristics that we admired. But He is not selfish with His possessions; He devised a plan that enables all to obtain exactly what He has. This plan caused such great happiness that we rejoiced exceedingly (see Job 38:7). The Father's plan of salvation involved us coming to Earth, experiencing opposition, and striving to make our way back to Him. Because of the difficulty involved, not all will choose to return. I'm certain the thought of losing any of His children is heartbreaking for Heavenly Father, but He knows that the only way for us to truly become like Him is to give us the options of obedience and disobedience.

Lucifer was also eager to obtain all the Father has, but he didn't want to hassle with a mortal probation. His proposed plan would have forced everyone to be obedient, guaranteeing all of Father's children would return to their heavenly home, but Lucifer's plan would have completely eliminated the marvelous gift of moral agency. As payment for this proposed service, he demanded the Father's glory. Lucifer's plan was rejected, and due to his subsequent rebellion, he and his followers were cast out. His lofty goal of gaining all the Father has was forever frustrated. Moral agency was such a critical aspect of the Father's plan that He was willing to lose a third of His children to preserve this marvelous gift. Elder Dale G. Renlund of the Quorum of the Twelve Apostles taught,

> Our Heavenly Father's goal in parenting is not to have His children *do* what is right; it is to have His children *choose* to do what is right and ultimately become like Him. If He simply

wanted us to be obedient, He would use immediate rewards and punishments to influence our behaviors. But God is not interested in His children just becoming trained and obedient "pets" who will not chew on His slippers in the celestial living room. No, God wants His children to grow up spiritually and join Him in the family business.[23]

This life is not just about killing time until we die. We are here to become far better than we were when we left our Father's presence. Those changes cannot be forced; we have to choose them. We will not improve unless we desire something greater and set and achieve goals to help us reach that objective. As Elder Renlund stated, we are here to "grow up spiritually." Mortal parents help their children learn to walk, tie their shoes, identify colors and words, and so on and so on until their children are self-sufficient and can progress on their own. They cannot force their children to learn; at some point the children need to choose to engage in the process and take responsibility for their own development. Our eternal progression follows the exact same pattern. Heavenly Father helps us develop celestial characteristics such as faith, charity, diligence, obedience, and compassion. He will not force us to learn these things but will encourage, command, and reinforce to inspire our compliance. Ultimately, He wants us to be spiritually self-sufficient and "join Him in the family business." This process takes time, and Father in Heaven is very patient with our efforts. We just have to do our best.

Personal competence, the belief in one's ability to set and achieve goals, is not only a foundational construct of emotional resilience but is a foundational construct of eternal progression. With moral agency, we have both the power and the responsibility to set appropriate goals. Because of agency and the Savior's Atonement, we have access to strength to achieve those goals. Although mortal weakness complicates our progress, we can eventually move past that and develop daily practices that will help increase our skill of personal competence.

Thought Journal

What are two or three things you'd like to remember from this chapter?

---

23 Dale G. Renlund, "Choose You This Day," *Ensign*, November 2018, 104.

Case Study (Personal Competence): "Jennifer"

Jennifer is a twenty-eight-year-old mother of three. She met her husband when she was a sophomore in college. About eight months into their marriage, she became pregnant. She tried to continue her university studies and graduate, but with her husband being a full-time student and her responsibilities as a young mother, she found there just weren't enough hours in the day to get everything done. She and her husband determined it would be better for her to stop attending school until he graduated so she could focus on raising their son.

Just prior to her husband's graduation, Jennifer discovered she was pregnant again. She was very sick with this pregnancy. Although she had intended to resume schooling in the near future, she felt completely overwhelmed and chose to delay her decision. Years passed and they had another child. Jennifer now found herself in full-time motherhood, enjoying her experience but having periodic feelings of regret that she never finished her university education. Their family had since moved from the university setting, and she was plenty busy raising three young children. In time, Jennifer heard about the BYU Pathway program, with which she could earn a college degree from home. She was thrilled at this idea, believing it offered the flexibility she needed to finally finish what she had started many years ago.

She sought information about the degrees and planned a course of action. However, she quickly became overwhelmed with details. When would she find time to study? Would she adjust to the online learning model? Completing her degree would cost thousands of dollars; how could they afford that? As she considered the obstacles, Jennifer grew more and more discouraged. She devoted less and less energy to thinking about her goal, her children taking up all her spare time, and eventually stopped making any plans to complete her education.

Review the three roadblocks to personal competence (Misunderstanding Our Purpose, Procrastination, Lack of Sustained Effort) previously discussed in this chapter and answer the following questions.

- In your opinion, which of these roadblocks is preventing Jennifer from moving forward? It could be one or more.

- Describe how each roadblock you have identified prevents Jennifer from progressing toward her goal.

- Based on what you've learned in this chapter, what would be a helpful strategy (or strategies) for Jennifer to consider?

Resolution

After an encouraging talk with her husband and her friends, Jennifer decided to move forward. She realized she didn't need to do everything at once. This was a lofty goal that would possibly take years to complete. She could take her time, ensuring she would have enough energy and resources to complete each step. Jennifer also determined that she would start small, taking one class to begin with, and reevaluate her course on a regular basis.

Please see Appendix E for additional exercises for Chapter Five.

CHAPTER SIX
EMOTIONAL RESILIENCE ELEMENT #2: TENACITY

THOMAS EDISON WAS AN AMERICAN scientist who had an insatiable appetite for discovery. With over a thousand patents attributed to him, he is considered one of America's most prolific inventors. His creations include the incandescent light bulb and the phonograph. He closely supervised the development of the motion-picture camera. Edison also dramatically improved upon the existing inventions of the telegraph, telephone, and electrical batteries. Many of the technologies we commonly use today had their genesis in the genius of Thomas Edison. The story is told of his attempts to improve upon the battery, seeking a format for longer-lasting storage and power. His friend visited him at his workshop, finding the remnants of hundreds of experiments. This friend discovered that Edison had done more than *nine thousand* experiments to find an appropriate solution for the battery, but none had been effective. He grieved at Edison's chronic failures. The friend said to Edison,

> "Isn't it a shame that with the tremendous amount of work you have done you haven't been able to get any results?" Edison turned on [him] like a flash, and with a smile replied: "Results! Why, man, I have gotten a lot of results! I know several thousand things that won't work."[24]

Edison clearly possessed the emotionally resilient quality of tenacity. Tenacity can be defined as being determined and persistent, continuing to move forward despite obstacles. This is a key concept for enduring challenges, as it refers not only to one's ability to survive the difficulty but one's

---

24 Frank L. Dyer and Thomas C. Martin, *Edison: His Life and Inventions* (New York: Harper and Brothers, 1910), 616.

determination to continue working and eventually become stronger. As we've previously discussed, one of the primary purposes of trials is to help us grow. Lisa L. Harkness, former First Counselor in the Primary General Presidency, stated,

> In times of turmoil our faith can feel stretched to the limits of our endurance and understanding. Waves of fear can distract us, causing us to forget God's goodness, thus leaving our perspective short-sighted and out of focus. Yet it is in these rough stretches of our journey that our faith can be not only tried but fortified.[25]

Developing tenacity not only helps sustain us through challenges but can also increase our capacity to use adversity to improve emotional strength.

The ability to move on despite difficulty can be compromised when we believe our choices are limited. Often, we are faced with false dilemmas. A false dilemma is when we have a problem, see only a few potential solutions, and feel that none of them are desirable. Because all possible outcomes seem undesirable, we feel frustrated and often do nothing. The reason these situations are called *false dilemmas* is because there are actually more prospective options than we had previously considered. It takes creative thinking to see beyond limited choices and find ways to move forward.

Another story from the life of Thomas Edison helps illustrate the concept of tenacity in the face of false dilemmas and the value of creative thinking:

> During the process of the ore-milling work at Edison, it became desirable to carry on a certain operation by some special machinery. He [Thomas Edison] requested the proper person on his engineering staff to think this matter up and submit a few sketches of what he would propose to do. He brought three drawings to Edison, who examined them and said none of them would answer. The engineer remarked that it was too bad, for there was no other way to do it. Mr. Edison turned to him quickly, and said: "Do you mean to say that these drawings represent the only way to do this work?" To which he received the reply: "I certainly do." Edison said nothing. This happened on a Saturday. He followed his usual custom of

---

25 Lisa L. Harkness, "Peace, Be Still," *Ensign*, November 2020, 81.

spending Sunday at home in Orange. When he returned to the works on Monday morning, he took with him sketches he had made, showing FORTY-EIGHT other ways of accomplishing the desired operation, and laid them on the engineer's desk without a word. Subsequently one of these ideas, with modifications suggested by some of the others, was put into successful practice.[26]

In another example, once I heard an anecdotal account of a creative team at Walt Disney World charged with designing entertainment offerings. With the resort being in central Florida, rainy weather is often a challenge. While brainstorming ideas, the team had a single rule: no proposed idea could be dismissed out of hand but must be considered and discussed. As the group grappled with how to deal with shows in wet and soggy conditions, one of the members said, "What if we did a rain parade?" At first, the idea seemed ridiculous. Rain is what cancels and ruins parades. But because all ideas were to be explored, the concept was considered. The idea started to gain traction. Costume designers indicated they could develop water-resistant costumes and nonskid footwear. Merchandisers stated that they could have ponchos available for purchase. Engineers reported that they could create floats in which sensitive electrical systems were protected from moisture. The team ultimately developed a "rainy-day parade" that can be seen on occasion at the Magic Kingdom.

The engineer was faced with a false dilemma, as was Disney's creative team, but perhaps the engineer wasn't thinking creatively enough. His mindset, *There is only one way*, prevented him from seeing the possibilities Edison saw. It's clear that Edison had no such mindset, as he was able to come up with dozens of possible solutions to the problem compared to the engineer's three. Edison's drive to accomplish the project led to additional effort and expanded thinking, ultimately yielding results. Similarly, if the creative team at Disney had maintained the mindset, *You can't do parades in the rain*, they likely would have missed the opportunity to create rainy-day magic for their determined patrons and keep the park operational during less-ideal weather. Those without tenacity are likely to give up when faced with challenges; those with tenacity persist through difficulty and find ways to go around roadblocks.

The brother of Jared is another excellent example of tenacity. He was the spiritual leader of his people. After being reprieved from the confounding

---

[26] Dyer and Martin, *Edison*, 624–25.

of languages at the Tower of Babel, he and his followers were to travel to a promised land. Their journey led them to ocean shores, which presented a serious challenge. They needed to cross the sea to reach their destination. Fortunately, the Lord helped them. He instructed the brother of Jared to build watertight barges. This eliminated a significant obstacle, as they now had a way to navigate the sea and arrive at their new home, but upon further examination, they discovered the barges had two potential problems. The people had built them so skillfully that not only were they watertight, but they were airtight as well. In addition, they were pitch-black inside. The brother of Jared took his concerns to the Lord, who provided additional revelation:

> And the Lord said unto the brother of Jared: Behold, thou shalt make a hole in the top, and also in the bottom; and when thou shalt suffer for air thou shalt unstop the hole and receive air. And if it be so that the water come in upon thee, behold, ye shall stop the hole, that ye may not perish in the flood. (Ether 2:20)

This engineering design solved the suffocation problem.

They still had the problem of the barges having no light. The brother of Jared inquired again,

> O Lord, behold I have done even as thou hast commanded me; and I have prepared the vessels for my people, and behold there is no light in them. Behold, O Lord, wilt thou suffer that we shall cross this great water in darkness? (Ether 2:22)

Perhaps the brother of Jared expected the Lord to provide another ready-made solution, but no. The Lord's response was potentially vexing:

> And the Lord said unto the brother of Jared: What will ye that I should do that ye may have light in your vessels? For behold, ye cannot have windows, for they will be dashed in pieces; neither shall ye take fire with you, for ye shall not go by the light of fire. . . . Therefore what will ye that I should prepare for you that ye may have light when ye are swallowed up in the depths of the sea? (Ether 2:23, 25)

It's interesting that the Lord first told the brother of Jared what he *couldn't* do: they were not to use windows or fire to create light. That effectively eliminated all light sources he was familiar with. Despite this, the brother of Jared was asked to come up with an alternative way to get light in the barges. Talk about a dilemma! I wonder what went through his mind during this interesting time. Here are some possible ideas:

- Option one: We can just give up now. We are at a beautiful beach and could live here happily for the rest of our lives.
- Option two: We can make the journey in darkness. It would be miserable and terrifying but ultimately possible.
- Option three: We can come up with a different option.

Fortunately, the brother of Jared chose option three. It required significant thinking outside of the box. He created sixteen transparent stones. Then, in humble prayer, he asked the Lord to touch the stones and make them shine. His request was granted. Not only did he receive divinely powered light sources, but he also got the incomparable blessing of seeing the premortal Jehovah (see Ether 3). Note the sequence of events in this process. There was a problem with no readily available solution. Instead of giving up, the brother of Jared persisted. He came up with an idea that required both his own work *and* heavenly intervention to succeed. He was blessed with the answer to his problem in addition to a faith-building reward.

Can you see how that same pattern could play out in your life as you face problems? The key in this scenario was tenacity: being determined and persistent and continuing to move forward despite obstacles. Some days, being tenacious may be beyond your emotional capacity. But as you aspire to develop greater tenacity, you'll find ways to act and grow as you are able. The very process of continuing to work toward a difficult goal despite opposition is the building of tenacity.

Let's discuss some of the things that can get in the way of developing tenacity in our lives:

Roadblock #1: Fear of Failure

Sometimes we don't persist due to fear that we won't succeed. It's the strategy of avoiding loss by never entering the contest. While that plan may seem effective, not getting into the game is basically a guaranteed form of loss. Let's say you have the possibility of a promotion at work but only if you apply for it. If you apply for the promotion, there are two potential outcomes: you get the promotion (success) or you do not get the promotion (failure). If you do not apply for the promotion, there is one guaranteed outcome: you don't get the promotion. The very thing you feared becomes a certain reality if you don't try. With that understanding, if we are truly afraid of failure, we should *always* try because that at least gives us a fighting chance not to fail. Tenacity involves risking failure, which is why those who fear failure may not persist when the going gets tough. In my experience, failure is unavoidable. No matter how hard we try, no matter how ingenious our schemes, failure is bound to result at least some of the time. But failure is a great teacher and can help us grow if we see it as an ally instead of an enemy. If we learn to tolerate failure as an acceptable outcome, we will develop greater ability to endure setbacks.

Roadblock #2: Rigid Thinking

When I was in graduate school, I did original research for my master's thesis in which I investigated the relationship between various personal characteristics and mental health conditions. I found a significant positive relationship between dogmatism (which is basically inflexibility of thought) and negative mental health indicators such as anxiety and depression. Rigid thinking can be a significant obstacle to tenacity. For example, the rigid thinker will encounter a problem and craft a solution. They implement the solution but then discover an unexpected obstacle. Their original solution no longer works because of the obstacle. Due to their inability to think flexibly, they are unable to come up with an alternative strategy and have to abandon the task. If the brother of Jared had been a rigid thinker, he would not have come up with the ingenious and unconventional idea of creating stones and asking God to make them glow. Life's challenges are fluid, constantly moving and adjusting. We need a similar approach to be successful. Developing greater flexibility in thinking can help us find novel solutions and stronger motivation to persist despite difficulty. The very act of reading this book and considering alternative ideas will help you become more flexible in thought; you are making progress as you read.

Roadblock #3: Lack of Self-Confidence

It goes without saying that if we don't believe in ourselves, we will experience far greater stress when faced with challenges. In the spectacular musical

Hadestown, the protagonist Orpheus is tasked with rescuing his beloved Eurydice from Hades. He bargains with the devil to take her from hell, but the devil imposes two conditions. First, the lovers must walk single file back to the earth, Orpheus taking the lead. Second, Orpheus is not permitted to look behind to see if Eurydice is still following. So he must make the long, dangerous walk, having faith that she is close behind him but never being able to make certain. The journey goes well until the Fates get into his head. They taunt that he could never accomplish something so difficult and dangerous. They question his capacity to win against the mighty Hades. Orpheus starts to question himself, doubting his abilities. How could he, a simple peasant, outwit the king of the underworld? His doubts get the best of him. What Orpheus lacks in self-confidence eventually leads to his downfall.[27] Self-confidence is a significant contributor to tenacity. When we face obstacles, those with conviction will believe in their ability to find a way and subsequently accomplish their designs.

Chapter Six Exercise

Here is an opportunity for you to examine something specific in your life, to determine possible approaches to increase your skill of tenacity.

Consider a chronic challenge you face. It could be external or internal. Write down at least three strategies you can use to overcome the challenge.

Pick one of the strategies you identified and answer the following questions:

- What is something you can do on a regular basis to help you implement that strategy?

- What is something you can do *today* to help you implement that strategy?

---

[27] *Hadestown* by Anaïs Mitchell, dir. Rachel Chavkin, Walter Kerr Theater, New York, NY, July 31, 2019.

Developing tenacity is not a short-term project. By its very nature, it takes years to achieve fully. Being patient and persistent in the development of any skill by working toward a goal and overcoming obstacles along the way also results in increased tenacity. Improved tenacity is often a side effect of faithfully trying to move forward. Nevertheless, we should be intentional about developing this characteristic, having been commanded to expand our capacity to endure. In his closing words, Nephi, son of Lehi, spoke of the doctrine of Christ. He taught how faith in Jesus Christ and repentance were essential foundational steps. These pave the way for baptism by immersion for the remission of sins, followed by receiving the supportive and sanctifying gift of the Holy Ghost. Such principles and ordinances get us on the path and set the stage for the final step, which is the most significant in terms of our overall spiritual development:

> And now, my beloved brethren, after ye have gotten into this strait and narrow path, I would ask if all is done? Behold, I say unto you, Nay . . . ye must press forward with a steadfastness in Christ, having a perfect brightness of hope, and a love of God and of all men. Wherefore, if ye shall press forward, feasting upon the word of Christ, and endure to the end, behold, thus saith the Father: Ye shall have eternal life. (2 Nephi 31:19–20)

Enduring to the end surely involves tenacity. It requires doing our best to be strong throughout temptations, trials, and troubles. It entails flexible thinking and a humble, obedient heart.

Alma the Younger was both a Nephite prophet and the chief judge, occupying the highest spiritual and political roles of his day. He abdicated his responsibilities as chief judge in order to give full attention to his spiritual and religious responsibilities. He then embarked on a tour of the land, preaching truth to help Church members either remain faithful or return to faithfulness. He enjoyed varying degrees of success, sometimes substantial, until he reached the city of Ammonihah. In that city, he fasted and prayed and preached with great effort but was wholly rejected by the people. Ultimately, he was cast out, having done his best. One could assume the Lord was satisfied with Alma's labor, for it appears Alma had given it his all. As he retreated dejectedly from Ammonihah, he was met by an angel. It was the same angel who appeared to him and the sons of Mosiah at the beginning of their conversion. This time, the angel had good news.

Blessed art thou, Alma; therefore, lift up thy head and rejoice, for thou hast great cause to rejoice; for thou hast been faithful in keeping the commandments of God from the time which thou receivedst thy first message from him. (Alma 8:15)

But the angel wasn't there to simply bless Alma for his good work; there was more to be done. The angel continued. "And behold, I am sent to command thee that thou return to the city of Ammonihah, and preach again unto the people of the city; yea, preach unto them. Yea, say unto them, except they repent the Lord God will destroy them" (Alma 8:16).

This presented an interesting situation for Alma. He had *just left* the city, having been rejected in no uncertain terms, feeling quite depressed about the outcome. There were significant obstacles to preaching the gospel in Ammonihah, and Alma had probably encountered all of them. Then the angel commanded him to return and preach again. What would you do? What thoughts would come to mind at such a request? *Doesn't the Lord know they already rejected me? I tried everything; nothing worked. It will just be a waste of time to continue. They are a lost people. I should find other cities that will be more receptive.* Those are all valid, rational thoughts. Alma had already demonstrated tenacity by preaching to these people for as long as he did. But what did he do? "Now it came to pass that after Alma had received his message from the angel of the Lord *he returned speedily* to the land of Ammonihah" (Alma 8:18; emphasis added).

He didn't wait. He didn't delay. Alma likely ran back to the city, to the very jaws of adversity that he had only recently escaped. If you are looking for an excellent practical example of tenacity, *this is it*. There were complications galore, but Alma trusted in God and looked for ways to prevail. I realize many may think, *That's a great example, but I'm no Alma the Younger*. Don't worry; in the Lord's plan, we get credit for trying. Try to see such examples as models of potential growth, rather than something you need to be like right away. As you work to increase skills of tenacity or continue to move forward despite challenges, you can build emotional resilience. This is done through your persistent efforts and through the Savior's grace. Remember the lessons taught in chapter four regarding the enabling power of the Atonement of Jesus Christ. This power will provide you with additional strength beyond your natural capacities, helping you face challenges and persevere despite obstructions or obstacles. As you do your part and rely on the Lord for His strengthening influence, you will develop skills to move forward despite the headwinds of adversity.

Thought Journal

What are two or three things you'd like to remember from this chapter?

Case Study (Tenacity): "Roger"

Roger is a twenty-four-year-old single man. He served a mission for The Church of Jesus Christ of Latter-day Saints and has been home for three years. As he left missionary service, his mission president encouraged him to date and seek marriage. Roger took that counsel seriously and started dating shortly after he returned home. However, he found there were few compatible people to date in his small town. When he went to college, he was excited about the potential dating pool. Yet, after months and months of first dates with no real connections, Roger decided to stop dating for a while and focus on his education.

A couple of years passed, and Roger didn't date at all. He socialized with friends on occasion but spent significant time alone as well. He started to grow more and more comfortable with his level of social interaction, making it easier not to date. However, he had nagging feelings from the counsel of his mission president in addition to counsel he'd received since that time from other priesthood leaders. Roger felt the Spirit directing him to start dating again, even though it would be difficult. He took the challenge and began going to more social events, getting involved on dating apps, and looking for other opportunities to meet young women. Eventually he found someone named Lisa who caught his interest. Lisa and Roger had common backgrounds, as she was raised in the area where he served his mission. They shared similar interests. She and Roger started chatting online and developed a friendship.

In time, Lisa and Roger went on a date and really enjoyed each other's company. They started dating frequently and then exclusively. In Roger's mind, things were going very well. He began thinking about marriage but was hesitant to bring this up to Lisa. He wasn't sure how she felt about it and was worried she might feel he was coming on too strong. But his thoughts of marriage did not go away, and he decided to address the subject. On their next date, he said, "I've been thinking about our relationship and am really happy with the way it is going. Maybe we can talk about what happens from here." Lisa said that would be fine but indicated she'd like to talk about it another time. The next day, Roger texted her. She didn't respond. He texted a few hours later and still got no response. A day later with still no reply to his texts, he started to worry. Was he being rejected? Had he misread their relationship? He wanted to call her but feared she was no longer interested. He did not want to face that possibility.

Review the three roadblocks to tenacity (Fear of Failure, Rigid Thinking, Lack of Self-Confidence) previously discussed in this chapter.

- In your opinion, which of these roadblocks is preventing Roger from moving forward? It could be one or more.

- Describe how each roadblock you have identified prevents Roger from progressing.

- Based on what you've learned in this chapter, what would be a helpful strategy (or strategies) for Roger to consider?

Resolution

Roger spent some time pondering and praying about what to do. He talked with a good friend, who helped him see that he might be overthinking the situation. Lisa clearly had feelings for him, and they had a good relationship. Roger reflected on his emotions and realized he was so afraid of being rejected that he was not taking the risk to move forward. He ultimately determined he would remain stuck unless he took action, despite his fears. Roger called Lisa; she answered. They had a good conversation about their relationship and future plans.

Please see Appendix F for additional exercises for Chapter Six.

CHAPTER SEVEN
EMOTIONAL RESILIENCE ELEMENT #3: ACCEPTANCE OF THE STRENGTHENING EFFECTS OF STRESS

The Church of Jesus Christ of Latter-day Saints has produced many short videos entitled *Inspirational Messages* (formerly *Mormon Messages*). They are excellent and cover a range of topics. One of my favorites is called "The Refiner's Fire."[28] The video begins by showing a blacksmith with an ordinary metal rod. He stokes a fire and heats the metal until it turns red, then twists, smashes, and bends it into a new shape. The story transitions to a woman who tells a compelling story. While their family was still young, she and her husband discovered their twenty-two-month-old son had a cancerous tumor. Despite multiple medical interventions, the child died. Later, their daughter was diagnosed with bone cancer. Then her husband contracted Burkitt's lymphoma. Tragically, another son was diagnosed with cancer as well. Although the daughter survived, the son died. Three weeks later, this woman's husband died as well. Throughout the video, as the woman is telling her story, the scene cuts back to the blacksmith as he essentially tortures the metal rod to change its shape. He ultimately transforms it into a beautiful rose. It is a persuasive metaphor to describe the intense suffering endured by this woman. She talks about how she was changed through her challenges. Notably, she reports how she is now better able to help others who suffer with cancer because of her experiences. Not only was she strengthened because of her personal agony but she also developed true compassion that can bless the lives of others.

Learning to accept the strengthening effects of stress is a pillar of emotional resilience. The only way to become stronger is to endure stress of some kind. Think about it: if you want to become stronger but never endure any stress, you will remain weak. The homely metal rod that wants to become a beautiful

---

[28] "The Refiner's Fire," *Mormon Messages*, churchofjesuschrist.org/inspiration/latter-day-saints-channel/watch/series/mormon-messages/the-refiners-fire?lang=eng. Accessed November 11, 2020.

wrought-iron flower must undergo stress and strain to endure the transformation. Note that there is a difference between learning to accept the strengthening effects of stress and loving every minute of stressful experiences. We don't need to enjoy pain. We *do* need to understand that periodic stress is okay and can be resiliently endured instead of avoided. Adopting this mindset will result in two beneficial outcomes. First, it will reduce emotional distress when times get tough. If you are of the opinion that all stress is bad, then when you encounter stress, you will automatically experience a double portion. You'll have the strain of the stressful event *plus* the added worry about the fact that you are going through stress. In other words, *you are stressing about being stressed*. That's too much and completely needless. If you believe some stress can be beneficial and lead to good outcomes, then when stress comes, you won't be unnecessarily alarmed. Second, the belief that *certain* stressors can be good will encourage you to endure. Instead of trying to avoid the stressor, you'll engage and do your best to succeed. This leads to greater emotional strength that will help with future trials.

Unfortunately, stress is often considered a negative concept. As a society, we invest considerable resources to address it. Particular strategies can help us learn how to deal with stress. I once received a weekly email that taught various techniques to remain calm and handle challenges. I found it very helpful. Other strategies are less helpful, as they are designed to help us avoid or ignore stress through distraction or numbing. Some of these strategies can be very damaging. For example, in my professional life, I've worked with thousands of individuals who have abused substances to temporarily decrease stress. This approach fixes nothing, creates more problems, and results in tragedy. Other strategies are not so much damaging as they are ultimately unhelpful. Many times in my personal life, when faced with stressful situations, I have turned to distractions such as surfing the internet, watching television, or engaging in some other mindless activity. While I get a temporary respite, the result is always the same: the stress is still there afterward and will remain until I deal with it or it resolves on its own. There is nothing inherently bad about this approach; it is simply a distraction that does not get us anywhere. If we want to move forward, we ultimately need to address the stressor and do what we can to cope with or resolve it appropriately. Trying to avoid all stressors does not truly work, as life is filled with challenges and setbacks. Despite our best efforts, there will always be times when our peace is disrupted by an unexpected turn of events.

Michael J. Fox is a Canadian-American actor who achieved fame as the conservative son of liberal parents in the television sitcom *Family Ties*. He was rocketed into superstardom when he played the role of Marty McFly in the *Back to the Future* movie series. At twenty-nine years of age (in approximately 1990), he was diagnosed with Parkinson's disease, a neurodegenerative disorder that causes multiple motor problems. It is extremely rare to be diagnosed with Parkinson's disease at such a young age. In the coming years, Michael's physical problems intensified to the point where he had to retire from full-time acting. He has spent decades searching for a cure and helping others who suffer from this crippling condition. In 2018 his doctors discovered he had an extremely painful but noncancerous spinal tumor. The tumor was surgically removed, but Michael had to spend months learning to walk again. Shortly after his recovery, he fell in his kitchen and broke his arm. He told a reporter,

> I just snapped. I was leaning against the wall in my kitchen, waiting for the ambulance to come, and I felt like, "This is as low as it gets for me." It was when I questioned everything. Like, "I can't put a shiny face on this. There's no bright side to this, no upside. This is just all regret and pain."[29]

Such a situation sure seems like adding insult to injury. His amazing acting career was short-circuited by an extremely rare medical circumstance, he developed a spinal tumor, and then had barely learned to walk again when he broke an arm. There are probably few who understand that level of stress. Yet Michael adjusted his attitude with admirable resilience. He stated, "Parkinson's, my back, my arm . . . it still didn't add up to moving the needle on the misery index compared to what some people go through. I thought, 'How can I tell these people, "Chin up. Look at the bright side. Things are going to be great"?'"[30] He then made a significant statement that highlights how accepting stress and difficulty can potentially be strengthening:

> Optimism is really rooted in gratitude. Optimism is sustainable when you keep coming back to gratitude, and what follows from that is acceptance. Accepting that this thing has happened, and you accept it for what it is. It doesn't mean that you can't endeavor to change. It doesn't mean you have

---

[29] Kate Coyne and Ally Mauch, "Michael J. Fox Reveals Painful Setback That Led to His 'Darkest Moment' Since Parkinson's Diagnosis," *People*, November 4, 2020, people.com/tv/michael-j-fox-reveals-the-painful-setback-that-led-to-his-darkest-moment-since-parkinsons-diagnosis/. Accessed November 22, 2020.
[30] Coyne and Mauch, "Michael J. Fox Reveals Painful Setback."

to accept it as a punishment or a penance, but just put it in its proper place. Then see how much the rest of your life you have to thrive in, and then you can move on.[31]

When we view stress as a growth opportunity, our attitude can improve, and we become more willing to accept challenges. Abinadi was a Book of Mormon prophet who was called to preach repentance to a wayward people. He boldly testified of the people's wickedness, particularly evil King Noah's, but achieved little success. Eventually the king sought his life, and Abinadi went into hiding. Two years later, he returned among the people and resumed his prophetic charge. I have always been interested in that two-year period. The scriptures record nothing about it except to refer to the time frame. Abinadi had already been completely rejected by the people, who clearly had no interest in listening to or heeding his message. He had endured significant stress by preaching his unpopular sermons. One could argue that Abinadi had already fulfilled the Lord's command of calling the people to repentance, yet he returned to service. We don't know why he returned, but now his resolve was rock solid. He walked right back into the stressful situation and started preaching anew. This time he did not escape the king's clutches and was taken into custody.

After a miraculous presentation before King Noah and his priests, Abinadi was incarcerated for several days while the royal court deliberated his fate. They decided he was guilty of blasphemy and worthy of death. The king accused Abinadi,

> For thou hast said that God himself should come down among the children of men; and now, for this cause thou shalt be put to death unless thou wilt recall all the words which thou hast spoken evil concerning me and my people. (Mosiah 17:8)

The prophet had a choice: he could continue his stressful mission and risk possible death or simply recant his accusations and spare his life. I can think of many reasons to recant. Perhaps Abinadi was married; perhaps he had children. Would he leave them? Hadn't he already valiantly fulfilled the Lord's command? Surely there were many others who could benefit from his ministry if he were to be spared. All it would take was a simple denial—a little white lie that could literally save his life. But Abinadi's steadfastness was not negotiable. He boldly replied,

---

31 Coyne and Mauch, "Michael J. Fox Reveals Painful Setback."

> I say unto you, I will not recall the words which I have spoken unto you concerning this people, for they are true; and that ye may know of their surety I have suffered myself that I have fallen into your hands. Yea, and I will suffer even until death, and I will not recall my words, and they shall stand as a testimony against you. And if ye slay me ye will shed innocent blood, and this shall also stand as a testimony against you at the last day. (Mosiah 17:9–10)

His words angered the king, who ordered his death by fire. Abinadi submitted to the flames, sealing his testimony with his blood.

Why would he do this? Because he saw the benefit. He knew it was better for him to pass through difficulty, even if it meant death, to achieve the promised blessings that come because of obedience. He had multiple opportunities to avoid the stress. He could have refused the Lord's initial call to serve; he could have not returned after the two-year hiatus; he could have retracted his words and avoided a fiery death. But avoiding the stress at any point would have resulted in fewer chances to develop strength. In order to grow, he had to endure the stress and persist despite difficulty. Developing greater resilience means learning to look differently at stress and trials. I'm certain Abinadi did not relish the opportunity to burn at the stake but knew it was the best choice in his limited set of options. When we see stress as a chance for growth, we will approach it differently than if we see it as only a trial.

Let's talk about some common roadblocks that might encourage us to resist stress instead of accepting its strengthening potential.

Roadblock #1: Viewing All Trials as Negative

When we think of blessings, we tend to consider overtly positive things, like good health, a financial upturn, or smooth sailing through life. Such things are certainly favorable but perhaps represent an overly simplistic view of what it means to be blessed. What if blessings are not so much determined by our current circumstance but by the ultimate result? For example, could illness be a blessing if it helps one develop greater compassion? Could unemployment be a blessing if it leads to increased education and a better job? Think of the ancient prophet Joseph. Was it a blessing that he was sold into slavery by his brothers? That stressful turn of events led to the entire house of Israel being spared from the famine. I'm not suggesting that all difficulty is a potential blessing, yet if we believe blessings have to be fortunate and without stress, we might be blinded to a multitude of favors the Lord has extended to us. Viewing a trial as a blessing will encourage us to endure and embrace, coping with the stress instead of trying to eliminate or avoid it.

Roadblock #2: Viewing All Distress as Unacceptable

Sometimes the very thought of being in distress is enough to make us cringe. As our circumstances have become more and more blessed, we seem to have developed lower tolerance for stress. Modern technologies have created wonderful conveniences that enhance our lives, but they have come at a cost. Pioneer farmers had to wait months for a harvest; we can simply drive to a store to choose from a wide variety of food. Chronic aversion to stress or discomfort can lead to decreased emotional resilience. We must endure distress in order to improve; it is a spiritual and physical truth. Think about physical health: getting stronger muscles requires difficult exercise, periodic pain, and gradual rebuilding. Tolerating distress eventually leads to greater strength. If we avoid all physical stress, our muscles will weaken and eventually become rather useless. The same pattern applies to emotional and spiritual muscles. Avoiding emotional and spiritual stress will ultimately result in weakened emotional and spiritual capacities. Stress is not pleasant, but a certain amount is critical to developing emotional resilience.

Roadblock #3: Believing that Obedience Leads to Stress-Free Outcomes

There is a cultural belief among Latter-day Saints that if we are sufficiently obedient, we will not experience serious difficulties. I think that must simply be wishful thinking because I cannot find a shred of evidence for this concept in ancient or modern scripture. In fact, the opposite seems to be true. The faithful are often subjected to extreme trials, multiple difficulties filling their lives with stress and strain. Consider the lives of past and present Church leaders; they have endured significant challenges notwithstanding their faithfulness. Of course, trials are part of the heavenly plan to refine and purify our souls. But if we hold to the mistaken belief that the straight and narrow path is free of trouble, then our view of stress becomes skewed. With such a belief, if we encounter a stressful situation, we might think, *Something must be wrong. I must have screwed up. I need to take action to escape this uncomfortable circumstance.* However, the opposite is often true. "For whom the Lord loveth he chasteneth, and scourgeth every son whom he receiveth" (Hebrews 12:6). Encountering stress does not necessarily mean something is wrong with us or that we have been unfaithful. It could mean something is very right. Individual inspiration will help you determine the nature of any particular stressor, but we should not automatically assume that experiencing difficulty is the direct result of disobedience. Staying on the covenant path almost always involves challenges and their associated stress. We should embrace that stress with the knowledge that it will help us grow closer to God.

Chapter Seven Exercise

Here is an opportunity for you to examine something specific in your life to determine possible approaches to help you accept the strengthening effects of stress.

- Consider a *past* stressful situation, one that has already fully resolved. Describe that experience.

- Write down two ways in which that experience blessed your life.

- Now consider a *current* stressful situation, one that has not yet resolved. Describe that experience.

- Write down two ways in which this experience might ultimately bless your life.

You may have found it easier to write about the blessings associated with your past experience; hindsight allows us to see more clearly. But learning to see blessings *in the midst* of difficulty is an extremely valuable skill. It takes practice and focus. In November 2020 President Russell M. Nelson challenged people to take seven days and transform their social media posts into a daily gratitude journal. He encouraged us to think about those things we were grateful for and post them for others to see.[32] That week was one of the most enjoyable social media experiences I've ever had. Typically, when I scroll through my feeds, I see a mix of happiness, anger, frustration, and sadness. During that particular week, I was overwhelmed by seeing posts of thankfulness and appreciation. My finger got tired from liking almost every post I came across. What I found even more interesting was what was *not being* reported. I personally knew many of the people who were posting positive, thankful content. I knew their lives were not perfect. In many cases, I knew their lives had been turned upside down by various circumstances. They had every right to complain and post about those truly negative experiences, yet they chose to focus on the good; they chose to look for the blessings. In the midst of their trials, they sought the silver lining. Seeing stressful situations as potentially beneficial can help us remain positive during grief and develop greater faith in Jesus Christ.

Some difficulties come and find us; some people go looking for them. I readily admit I'm not the sort of person who regularly looks for a challenge to improve. But there are other, stronger people who know the value of trials and seek them out to improve their overall resilience. President Henry B. Eyring told of a memory of President Spencer W. Kimball. He reported that President Kimball actively sought for growth opportunities from the Lord, calling them "mountains to climb."[33] President Kimball wanted God to put such mountains in his path so he could gain spiritual strength. President Eyring was inspired by this and sought a similar experience:

---

32 Russell M. Nelson, "President Nelson on the Healing Power of Gratitude," *Church News*, November 11, 2020, thechurchnews.com/leaders-and-ministry/2020-11-20/president-nelson-special-message-gratitude-spiritual-remedy-healing-hope-covid-19-198180.
33 Henry B. Eyring, "Mountains to Climb," *Ensign*, May 2012, 23.

> My heart was stirred, knowing, as I did, some of the challenges and adversity [President Kimball] had already faced. I felt a desire to be more like him, a valiant servant of God. So one night I prayed for a test to prove my courage. I can remember it vividly. In the evening I knelt in my bedroom with a faith that seemed almost to fill my heart to bursting. Within a day or two my prayer was answered. The hardest trial of my life surprised and humbled me. It provided me a twofold lesson. First, I had clear proof that God heard and answered my prayer of faith. But second, I began a tutorial that still goes on to learn about why I felt with such confidence that night that a great blessing could come from adversity to more than compensate for any cost.[34]

I love the sequence of the Lord's intervention in President Eyring's example. First, the Lord blessed him with a reassurance of His love for President Eyring and His confidence in his abilities. Second, He administered the trial. Armed with self-assurance that he could prevail with God's help, President Eyring looked to the challenge with faith that any stress he would experience in the meantime would be completely eclipsed by the ultimate blessing. The Lord is so merciful! He provides tests but also supports us every step of the way. I have been through serious trials and have looked back to recognize the supporting hand of God throughout. The resultant blessings have been amazing. In some ways, it seems I have been unjustly favored. The trial came, my own efforts were insufficient, He strengthened me to succeed, and then He blessed me with such an abundance it felt as though I had vanquished the trial on my own. It doesn't seem fair to be so richly blessed from such meager efforts. I suppose it isn't fair or just at all; it is pure mercy. It is pure love. Accepting the strengthening effects of stress includes accepting the truth that Heavenly Father will never abandon us and will never introduce any difficulty into our lives that has greater potential for sorrow than joy.

Peter taught the ancient saints,

> Beloved, think it not strange concerning the fiery trial which is to try you, as though some strange thing happened unto you: But rejoice, inasmuch as ye are partakers of Christ's sufferings; that, when his glory shall be revealed, ye may be glad also with exceeding joy. (1 Peter 4:12–13)

---

[34] Henry B. Eyring, "Mountains to Climb."

Stress is going to happen in our lives. It can come from random events, the choices of others, our own decisions, or divine intervention. If we choose to face it, digging deep to endure and grow, it can become a source of strength instead of a stumbling block. As we adjust our mindset to accept stress as a potential vehicle for improvement, we can tolerate it better and develop stronger emotional resilience.

Thought Journal

What are two or three things you'd like to remember from this chapter?

Case Study (Acceptance of the Strengthening Effects of Stress): "Phil and Joann"

Phil and Joann are in their midforties and have been married for eighteen years. They have five children. The oldest is Jason, who is fifteen years of age. The family has been active in The Church of Jesus Christ of Latter-day Saints their entire lives. Phil and Joann come from faithful families, they both served missions for the Church, and they were married in the temple. They have faithfully attended church, magnified callings, and served others. In addition, they have been diligent about family prayer, scripture study, temple attendance, and other practices that have blessed their lives. In many ways, they are considered by their peers as model members of the Church.

One day, Phil was shocked to get a frantic call from Joann. She said while she was using the family computer, she received a pornographic spam email. Despite having filters in place, she found that additional software had been installed on the computer to enable web browsing without leaving an easily discovered trail. She suspected their son Jason, a computer whiz, might have been behind the issue. As she addressed the issue with their son, he'd tearfully confessed that he had installed the software, which had allowed him to look at pornography on a regular basis for the past six months.

Phil and Joann were beside themselves. What had they done wrong? How could they have let this happen? How could their son, whom they had loved and taught, have betrayed them this way? As they confronted their son in anger and frustration, Jason became even more tearful and angry. He said they didn't understand and he could never live up to their expectations, and he ran out of the room. Phil and Joann grieved at their situation and wondered how this could happen to their family despite their significant efforts to be obedient.

Review the three roadblocks previously discussed in this chapter (Viewing All Trials as Negative, Viewing All Distress as Unacceptable, Believing that Obedience Leads to Stress-Free Outcomes).

- In your opinion, which of these roadblocks is preventing Phil and Joann from moving forward? It could be one or more.

- Describe how each roadblock you have identified prevents Phil and Joann from progressing.

- Based on what you've learned in this chapter, what would be a helpful strategy (or strategies) for Phil and Joann to consider?

Resolution

After much fasting, prayer, and consultation with a counselor, Phil and Joann understood that their situation was more common than they realized. They stopped focusing on how they had been hurt by their son's actions and started focusing on how they could help him move forward. As they counseled together regarding the Savior's Atonement, they realized that the same saving power that could help their son deal with his pornography issues could also help them have greater peace regarding the situation. Jason ultimately decided to seek counseling and talk with his bishop.

Please see Appendix G for additional exercises for Chapter Seven.

CHAPTER EIGHT
EMOTIONAL RESILIENCE ELEMENT #4: TOLERANCE OF NEGATIVE AFFECT

IN 2017 THE UNITED STATES Department of Health and Human Services declared a public health emergency regarding the abuse of opioid medications.[35] It was in reaction to a problem that began decades earlier, resulting in what has been referred to as the opioid epidemic. Opioids are a class of drug that include powerful prescription painkillers. In the late 1990s there was a significant surge in use of these medications. One of the reasons for the increased use was that some pharmaceutical companies reassured the United States government that these medicines had low potential for abuse and dependence. Being very effective at reducing pain and with apparently little risk of addiction, they were widely prescribed for all sorts of uncomfortable conditions. It wasn't until many years later that it was discovered these drugs were highly addictive, were being overprescribed, and were being used illegally on a widespread basis. In addition, there have been many fatalities from improper use. Data from 2019 indicated that almost 50,000 people died from opioid-involved overdoses that year alone in the United States.[36]

Several years ago, I was in a conference that focused on addictions. One of the presentations was regarding a pain management treatment center. The center's philosophy was that the liabilities of opioids for pain management outweighed the benefits. The center had treated thousands of opioid-addicted patients with their innovative system. Many of their patients had a history of increased addiction that followed a consistent pattern:

- The patient sustained some injury or condition that caused chronic pain and sought medical treatment.

---

[35] "What Is the Opioid Epidemic?", U.S. Department of Health and Human Services, hhs.gov/opioids/about-the-epidemic/index.html. Accessed October 15, 2021.
[36] "Opioid Overdose Crisis," *National Institutes of Health*, drugabuse.gov/drug-topics/opioids/opioid-overdose-crisis. Accessed October 6, 2021.

- The medical professional prescribed an initial course of opioid medication therapy.
- The patient returned on occasion, reporting the effectiveness of the therapy.
- The medical professional asked, "On a scale of zero to ten, where zero is none and ten is a maximum level, how much pain do you experience on a daily basis?"
- If the patient responded anything higher than zero, the medical professional typically increased the opioid medication dosage.
- This process repeated until the patient ultimately became addicted to the opioid.

This particular program was designed to help with pain management *not* involving the use of opioids. When a person was accepted into the program, the first step was to safely take them off *all* opioid medications. Other treatments were introduced, including acupuncture, meditation, cognitive-behavioral therapy, yoga, and other nonmedicinal interventions. What interested me was how the patients handled the experience of pain. This clinic also used the zero-to-ten scale to have the patient rate their pain, but their approach was different from that of the doctors who had prescribed the opioids. The patients were asked, "On a scale of zero to ten, how much pain are you willing to live with?" I thought it was a brilliant question. In almost every case, the patient responded with a nonzero answer. Usually, their answers were in the range of two to four. That meant they were willing to live with a certain amount of pain and distress; they just didn't want that level to be a nine or ten. The various treatments and interventions used at the clinic were successful in helping many patients reduce their pain to a personally acceptable level.[37]

I found it fascinating that when these same patients were trying to achieve zero pain, they were constantly thwarted and had to increase their medication dosage over and over, yet when they decided there was a certain degree of pain they were willing to live with, they were able to find suitable relief without resorting to addictive chemicals. This relates to the principle of emotional resilience known as tolerance of negative affect. In this case, *affect* means an emotion or feeling. This principle describes to what degree we are willing to tolerate or endure negative feelings or emotions. It is similar to principle three,

---

37 Mel Pohl, "A Day Without Pain: Clinical Issues in the Treatment of Pain, Suffering, and Drug Dependence" (keynote presentation, 22nd Annual Northwest Conference on Behavioral Health and Addictive Disorders, Bellevue, Bellevue, WA, May 28, 2009.

accepting the strengthening effects of stress. It is also a variation of tenacity. Tenacity involves persisting at a task even when it becomes difficult. However, that task may be generally enjoyable. For example, I love to ride my bicycle and will sometimes take rides of up to fifty miles. The last ten miles of the ride require tenacity because although I enjoy the ride, I'm tired and eager to get home. In contrast, tolerating negative affect is when we are faced with a situation we do not enjoy, yet the situation persists; instead of fleeing the feeling, we choose to experience and work our way through the feeling. Sometimes people describe this as "sitting with" the feeling. One could even describe it as "emotional inoculation." A medical inoculation introduces a form of disease into the body so the immune system can learn to deal with and fight against it. Once inoculated, when the body encounters the same disease in the future, it is able to ward the disease off. Emotions work similarly. When we experience anger, anxiety, depression, etc., and we immediately try to escape such feelings, we develop no strength to deal with them. If we learn to tolerate these feelings, sitting with them for a time and learning how to adapt, we can gain emotional strength to cope with them in the future.

One of my favorite movies is *Batman Begins*. It tells the origin story of how Bruce Wayne became Batman. Early in the movie, a young Bruce falls into a deep, dry well, breaking his arm. The well is connected to a bat-infested cave. Not only is the young boy scared and hurt from his fall, but he also gets traumatized by hundreds of bats that swarm around him until he is rescued by his father. From that time, Bruce has a fear of bats. Later in life, he returns to the cave to explore. As he enters, he turns on a flashlight only to again be accosted by hundreds of bats. Instead of fleeing, he slowly stands, closes his eyes, and remains still as the bats fly frantically around him. His fear of bats ends, he adopts their persona for his secret identity, and actually uses them as allies at a later point in the film. I'm not sure Bruce ever grows to *love* the company of bats, but he learns to tolerate the feelings their presence evokes. That happens because he resists the impulse to escape the cave and instead learns to cope with what has previously terrified him.[38]

One of the problems with tolerating negative emotions is that many of us have developed a limited capacity for negativity due to insufficient experience with it. For developed countries, technological advances have rendered circumstances so comfortable that common discomforts are quickly becoming a thing of the past. People used to have to make their own candles and burn

---

[38] *Batman Begins*, directed by Christopher Nolan (Burbank: Warner Brothers, 2005).

them to have light. Now we have modern, efficient lighting that is powerful and flexible to meet many of our needs. Consider the case of animals raised in captivity. They don't develop the survival skills displayed by their noncaptive counterparts. If food is scarce and predators abound, animals learn very quickly how to find resources and protect themselves. If food is abundant and threats nonexistent, they don't develop the same skills. That's fine as long as they live in captivity their entire lives, but if they ever have to try to survive in the wild, their future is grim. Human beings also need challenges and adversity to grow, especially when it comes to spiritual development.

Elder Jeffrey R. Holland spoke persuasively on this topic in the October 2020 general conference. He remarked about how, despite our most fervent prayers and sincere efforts, some difficulties persist. This is not a flaw in the plan or the result of an absentminded God but part of our Father in Heaven's glorious design to help us become like Him. A critical and unique doctrine to The Church of Jesus Christ of Latter-day Saints is that Heavenly Father was once as we are and we have the potential to become like Him. That process necessarily involves distress. If we choose to circumvent that distress, we miss essential chances for growth. Loosely quoting Elder Neal A. Maxwell, Elder Holland spoke hypothetically about the plea we have all been prone to make at times:

> Lord, give me all thy choicest virtues, but be certain not to give me grief, nor sorrow, nor pain, nor opposition. Please do not let anyone dislike me or betray me, and above all, do not ever let me feel forsaken by Thee or those I love. In fact, Lord, be careful to keep me from all the experiences that made Thee divine. And then, when the rough sledding by everyone else is over, please let me come and dwell with Thee, where I can boast about how similar our strengths and our characters are as I float along on my cloud of comfortable Christianity.[39]

I'm not certain there is such a thing as "comfortable Christianity." In order to become like the Savior, we must experience at least some of the things He did. Creating lives of pure comfort, free of distress, will never yield the resilient characteristics that will help us get through the trials of life. I'm not saying we should go looking for difficulty, but when it naturally finds us (and it will), we should not run in the opposite direction. Please note I speak specifically of *feelings* and not necessarily *situations*. For example, if one is the victim of abuse, they should not tolerate the situation in hopes that it

---

39 Jeffrey R. Holland, "Waiting on the Lord," *Ensign*, November 2020, 116.

will lead to growth. The principle of resilience is tolerance of negative *affect* and not necessarily tolerance of negative *circumstances*. In the case of abuse, the victim would do well to escape the abusive situation (the circumstance) if possible. Going forward, that same individual would do well to address and resolve the negative feelings (the affect) that came from the abuse, as opposed to avoiding the confrontation of that issue.

In my professional life, I have worked with thousands of individuals who suffer from anxiety. Panic disorder is a common affliction for many of them. This condition manifests in periodic panic or anxiety attacks characterized by sweating, shallow breathing, increased heart rate, and dizziness. Such attacks are often brought on by exposure to social situations such as crowded stores or enclosed spaces or by stressful settings such as job interviews or interpersonal confrontation. Having a panic attack is extremely distressing. Those who have had one usually avoid all situations that could lead to having another. However, this strategy is ineffective for long-term anxiety management. In order to learn to deal with anxiety, *we have to feel anxiety*. I often counsel people to do the very thing that causes them stress, but in small and controlled ways. If going into a crowded store causes a panic attack, then I recommend they go into a crowded store for one minute. After the minute is over, they can leave. But during that minute, they need to wait, experience the emotions, and sit with the distress. Over time, that minute can be increased to two, four, eight, and so on. Crowded stores will probably never be their preferred hangout, but eventually they can learn to tolerate them enough to shop without crippling anxiety. If that same person forever avoids a crowded store, they will never develop the ability to cope with the associated anxiety.

Let's discuss several roadblocks that prevent us from tolerating negative emotions.

Roadblock #1: Having a Pessimistic Outlook

Faith is a critical element in emotional resilience. It sustains us through difficulty with the hope that things will get better in time. One can often cope better with a negative situation knowing that a positive outcome is on the horizon. However, if that same person views the future as bleak and dark, then what benefit comes of enduring negative situations? If tomorrow will be full of nothing but pain and distress, then it makes perfect sense to avoid discomfort as much as possible. But tomorrow does not have to be miserable. What we do today *necessarily* changes what tomorrow will be like, for good or for bad.

For those who have made sacred covenants, the future has unlimited potential. Pessimism drags us down, leading to greater emotional turmoil and fueling the urge to escape from distress. Optimism leads to positivity, confidence, and courage. The future is truly unknown to all of us, which makes pessimism and optimism equal in terms of likely outcome. All that remains is for us to choose which outlook we want. Although such a choice is not easy, it is possible. I recommend optimism as a tool to increase faith and help us develop greater tolerance for negative situations.

Roadblock #2: Being Unaccustomed to Dealing with Difficulty

The more we do something, the easier it becomes. The less we do something, the more difficult it becomes. As a licensed psychologist with a natural aversion to yard work, I spend a lot of time behind a desk and little time in manual labor. I do get out and do necessary yard work from time to time, but I find my stamina is pretty low. I'm a little embarrassed to admit that one hour of raking leaves can be difficult. As I'm sweating, I often think about those individuals who do manual labor for a living. I say to myself, "They're so tough! They can go eight to ten hours without getting as tired as I do after one." Then I realize their physical stamina comes from doing hard things over and over. If I were to start working in the yard each day, my body would adjust over time, and I'd develop a greater capacity to endure. Emotional endurance is no different. If we constantly avoid distressing situations, our capacity to endure suffering will be small and quickly exhausted. The more we appropriately engage with stress, learning to sustain ourselves instead of avoid difficulty, the greater capacity we'll develop to tolerate negative situations.

Roadblock #3: Seeking Excessive Comfort

At times we seek too much comfort and ease, which decreases our potential exposure to challenges. This tendency is often found in certain parenting styles, at times referred to as "lawnmower" or "bulldozer" parenting. Such parents use their influence and resources to clear the path before their children, filling holes and razing obstacles so the children will not have to experience much difficulty on their journey. There was a significant scandal in 2019 that involved affluent parents paying an illegal college admissions broker to get their children admitted to competitive colleges. This broker arranged for admissions tests to be falsified and college athletics groups to create phony recruitments for these youth to skip the rigor typically associated with getting admitted to a prestigious university.[40] As a parent, I sympathize and believe that many of these individuals had their hearts in the right place. But creating too much convenience and comfort for our children will not prepare them for the world they will inevitably face. By the same token, if we spend our resources trying to make our own lives as comfortable as possible, discomfort will be unwelcome and extra challenging. We need a healthy balance of difficulty and ease in our lives in order to develop emotional strength.

As we tolerate negative emotions, we learn about them. We study how they affect us. We develop insight into the types of situations that cause them. This information can be helpful in eventually overcoming such feelings. When I recommend tolerating these emotions, I don't mean surrendering to them with hopeless acceptance. Too often we feel we cannot change negative personality characteristics, saying, "That's just the way I am." We argue that anxious people will always be anxious; angry people will always be angry. That is not true. But anxious people who always run from their anxiety are more likely to remain anxious than those who intentionally experience and analyze the feeling. The same is true for any negative emotion. We can always change. Sometimes it's extremely challenging and we make slow progress, but *we can always change.*

Chapter Eight Exercise

Here is an opportunity for you to examine something specific in your life, to determine possible approaches to help you increase tolerance for negative emotions.

Think of two negative emotions you do not find enjoyable. What are they? For each emotion, answer the following questions:

- What do you usually do to make that emotion go away?

---

[40] "Investigations of College Admissions and Testing Bribery Scheme," United States Department of Justice, justice.gov/usao-ma/investigations-college-admissions-and-testing-bribery-scheme. Accessed October 15, 2021.

- Do you feel that is a productive approach to dealing with that emotion? Why or why not?

For each *nonproductive* approach you listed above, list a more productive approach you could use to deal with that emotion.

Alma the Elder was the righteous leader of a diligent people. From all accounts, they kept their covenants and practiced principles of personal virtue. Even so, the Lord determined to test their faith through a significant trial (see Mosiah 23:21). They were taken into bondage by a cruel group of Lamanites, some of whom had particularly angry feelings toward Alma. The Lamanites enslaved the Nephites, subjecting them to intense manual labor. When the Nephites cried out in vocal prayer for deliverance, the Lamanites threatened them with death if they prayed again. Still, the now-silent Nephite prayers reached the ears of Heavenly Father, and He blessed them. "And now it came to pass that the burdens which were laid upon Alma and his brethren were made light; yea, the Lord did strengthen them that they could bear up their burdens with ease" (Mosiah 24:15). Note how their burdens were eased, but they were still in captivity. They still had to follow the orders of their masters. They had no freedom to pray vocally. Even though they were able to shoulder their loads with heavenly strength, they remained in the midst of a terrible situation. One could reason that these people, despite the blessing, still had a lot to complain about. But Mormon describes their attitude after the Lord eased their burdens, as follows: "They did submit *cheerfully and with patience* to all the will of the Lord" (Mosiah 24:15; emphasis added). This is an exceptional example of tolerance of negative affect or emotion. Sometimes it is all we can do to grit our teeth through difficulty, but we can aspire to increase in strength and eventually become like this people. Their situation was negative—being in bondage is terrible. But they did their best. They strived to have a good attitude and abide the negative circumstance. They were blessed for their endurance and eventually were miraculously delivered from bondage.

Learning to endure negative situations breeds great strength. The smooth road is pleasant, but it builds no grit. Rough roads are challenging, and those who travel such roads can develop much greater abilities. In 2017 United States Supreme Court Chief Justice John Roberts's son graduated from high school. Chief Justice Roberts delivered the commencement address. His excellent oration has come to be known as the "I wish you bad luck" speech. Here is an excerpt:

> Now the commencement speakers will typically also wish you good luck and extend good wishes to you. I will not do that, and I'll tell you why. From time to time in the years to come, I hope you will be treated unfairly, so that you will come to know the value of justice. I hope that you will suffer betrayal because that will teach you the importance of loyalty. Sorry to say, but I hope you will be lonely from time to time so that you don't take friends for granted. . . . I hope you'll be ignored so you know the importance of listening to others, and I hope you will have just enough pain to learn compassion. Whether I wish these things or not, they're going to happen. And whether you benefit from them or not will depend upon your ability to see the message in your misfortunes.[41]

It's almost as if Chief Justice Roberts had recently read 2 Nephi 2:11, wherein Lehi tells his son Jacob about the necessity of opposition in life. Seeing the "message in our misfortunes" is analogous to tolerating negative emotions. Seeing the value of suffering is a blessing. Learning how to understand and process negativity is infinitely more valuable than having a life in which opposition has been eliminated. When faced with difficulties, we should try to square our shoulders and do our best to move forward. Enduring the challenge can not only make us stronger emotionally but can also qualify us for heavenly blessings. As the Lord told Joseph Smith during one of the darkest times of his life,

> My son, peace be unto thy soul; thine adversity and thine afflictions shall be but a small moment; And then, if thou endure it well, God shall exalt thee on high; thou shalt triumph over all thy foes. (D&C 121:7–8)

---

[41] John Roberts, "I Wish You Bad Luck," *James Clear*, jamesclear.com/great-speeches/i-wish-you-bad-luck-by-john-roberts. Accessed November 27, 2020.

May we all have such hope and strength during personal times of darkness.

THOUGHT JOURNAL

What are two or three things you'd like to remember from this chapter?

CASE STUDY (TOLERANCE OF NEGATIVE AFFECT): "JESSE"

Jesse is a forty-two-year-old widower. His wife's death was tragic and unexpected. They had one child together, Tina, who is a teenager. Jesse has struggled with anxiety his entire life. His wife's death and her leaving him to raise their daughter on his own only compounded his anxiety. Much to his dismay, following his wife's death, he started to see anxiety symptoms in his daughter as well. These symptoms increased over time to the point where Tina did not want to go to school, did not want to attend church activities, and preferred to be home reading or playing video games. Jesse has become terrified that his daughter will turn out like him, having poorly managed chronic anxiety.

Jesse had been praying diligently for a way to help his daughter deal with her anxious feelings. While at work, he received a text message from her. It said she had received a call from a bishopric counselor in their ward, and she was freaking out. Jesse finished what he was doing and drove straight home to help his daughter. Tina related how the counselor had invited her to give a talk in sacrament meeting. The idea of this completely terrified her. Tina did not like being around crowds, did not like speaking in public, and was worried she would do something to make herself look stupid. Just the thought of having to give this talk caused a panic attack. As Jesse helped his daughter calm down, his mind raced with thoughts of what he should do in this situation.

Jesse's first impulse was to call the bishop directly. He could explain how Tina has anxiety and this request was way outside her comfort zone. Surely the bishop would understand. There were dozens of youth in the ward, many of them well-spoken, and it was unnecessary to ask Tina to speak when there were so many other options. However, the thought of being so direct caused his own anxieties to act up. Jesse then figured he could schedule a last-minute trip for that Sunday. If he and Tina were not in town, then she could respectfully decline and hopefully they wouldn't ask her again. At the same time, he knew that running away was not a healthy strategy. Jesse was conflicted about how to proceed.

Review the three roadblocks previously discussed in this chapter (Having a Pessimistic Outlook, Being Unaccustomed to Dealing with Difficulty, Seeking Excessive Comfort).

- In your opinion, which of these roadblocks is preventing Jesse from moving forward? It could be one or more.

- Describe how each roadblock you have identified prevents Jesse from progressing.

- Based on what you've learned in this chapter, what would be a helpful strategy (or strategies) for Jesse to consider?

Resolution

Jesse told Tina he would think about what to do and they could develop a strategy together. He reflected on his life and his own anxieties. He remembered the many times he had avoided stressful situations, only to find himself with less and less emotional stamina as time went on. Jesse felt impressed to do a scripture search on the topics of *faith* and *fear*. As he studied, he felt confident that he could help Tina alleviate some of her anxiety while still facing her fears. Jesse asked Tina, "Besides just not giving the talk, what would make you feel less anxious about this request?" After discussing various options, Tina indicated that if she would be permitted to just read her brief written testimony, with her father standing by her side, she could probably survive. They called the bishopric counselor with the proposal, and he warmly accepted and thanked Tina for her courage. Tina was able to successfully give her talk and afterward remarked to Jesse, "That wasn't as bad as I thought it was going to be."

Please see Appendix H for additional exercises for Chapter Eight.

CHAPTER NINE
EMOTIONAL RESILIENCE ELEMENT #5: ACCEPTING CHANGE

From the moment I saw the stage adaptation of Victor Hugo's novel *Les Misérables*, I fell in love with the characters and story. The tale chronicles the life of Jean Valjean, an honest man who was caught stealing food to save his dying nephew. After serving nineteen years on the chain gang, he is paroled. He is thrilled when released but soon has the crushing discovery that being a parolee, he will be branded as a thief. Because of this, he is unable to get suitable employment or even find a warm place to sleep. Seeking a new start, he breaks his parole and assumes a new identity, only to be hunted by his parole officer, known simply as Javert. Valjean repents of his crimes and lives an honorable life, but Javert sees him only as a hardened criminal who must pay for escaping from parole. After finding him, Javert tells Valjean that criminals can never change; they will always resort to thievery and manipulation to get what they want. Valjean sees himself differently, tells Javert he is a changed man, and escapes. Later in the play the two cross paths again in the midst of the French Revolution, but this time Valjean has the upper hand. Javert is discovered as a traitor by revolutionary students and has been condemned to death. Valjean is given the duty to execute his own parole officer. Javert boldly faces his fate, furious that this criminal has the upper hand. Suddenly, his world is turned inside out. Instead of killing Javert, however, Valjean secretly frees him. Not only that, Valjean tells Javert he is willing to return to jail and provides an address where Javert can find him once the battle is over. An incredulous Javert warns Valjean that he *will* find him and take him into custody, then flees for his life. Not long after, Valjean and Javert meet one last time. Valjean carries a badly wounded friend, rushing him to the hospital. Javert threatens to arrest Valjean on the spot, but Valjean pleads for mercy for the dying man's sake. Inexplicably, and to his own surprise, Javert lets Valjean go, telling him he will find and arrest him later. This act of clemency is too much for Javert to process; how could an officer of the law let a hardened criminal escape? How could mercy rob justice? The dissonance is too much for him to handle, and he commits suicide, plunging into the Seine River.[42]

Change is practically a constant force in our lives. One would think that with change being so consistent, it would be easy to accept and integrate. But the opposite is often true. Most of us have difficulty adjusting to life's variations. For others, stress pushes them to the point where it begins to affect their emotional stability. Javert is a case in point. He always views Valjean as a thief and believs thieves can never change. This creates so much rigidity in Javert's thinking that his mind practically breaks in half as he considers that a thief might actually be virtuous on occasion. Inflexibility of thought, or unwillingness to accept change, is a barrier to emotional resilience.

Sometimes we get so firmly set on a certain outcome that anything else becomes unacceptable, and we struggle when things do not go as we had hoped. We need to develop the ability to consider other potential outcomes, thinking outside the box, in order to cope with many of the trials we face. It's okay to have expectations for the future; we just need to be flexible in their implementation. We should look to the future and move forward with determination and purpose. In fact, the Lord has instructed that we should do this:

> For behold, it is not meet that I should command in all things; for he that is compelled in all things, the same is a slothful and not a wise servant; wherefore he receiveth no reward. Verily I say, men should be anxiously engaged in a good cause, and do many things of their own free will, and bring to pass much righteousness. (D&C 58:26–27)

Making plans is wonderful; problems result when we cannot modify plans in the face of change. Old Testament prophet Jonah is a poignant example of an individual who had difficulty accepting change.

Consistent with the Lord's ancient pattern, Jonah was called by God for a specific assignment. The task was to preach repentance to the wicked people of Nineveh. Nineveh was the capital of Assyria, one of Israel's most formidable enemies. No doubt Jonah was not eager to go to the heart of hostile territory to preach an unpopular message, but his assignment was clear. He had already

---

42 *Les Misérables* by Claude-Michel Schönberg and Alain Boublil, dir. by John Caird and Trevor Nunn, Curran Theater, San Francisco, CA, August 11, 1990.

done prophetic work in his local area (see 2 Kings 14:25), but this new duty would be a substantial change. Nineveh was more than seven hundred miles from Jonah's hometown, so not only was the task daunting but the journey was significant as well. Instead of going to Nineveh as commanded, Jonah fled. He went to the coastal town of Joppa and boarded a vessel bound for Tarshish, heading away from his assignment (see Jonah 1:3). Let's summarize Jonah's circumstance to this point, and his adaptation to the change introduced into his life:

- The situation: Jonah is living comfortably at home.
- The change: Jonah is called to leave home and preach to a wicked people.
- The reaction: Jonah runs away from the assignment.

The sailors on the boat had no idea he was trying to hide from God. To them, Jonah was just another passenger. They made sail and embarked on their journey. While Jonah's prophetic identity and heavenly call were hidden from his fellow shipmates, they were not hidden from the Lord. To thwart Jonah's retreat, God caused a terrible storm that threatened to destroy the ship. While the mariners panicked and dumped cargo into the sea, Jonah peacefully slept. He was awakened by the captain and asked to pray for relief. Jonah then disclosed that he was probably the reason for the storm, as he was essentially a spiritual fugitive. Without being able to get to land, and with the tempest threatening certain destruction, Jonah's solution was to eliminate the problem. "And he [Jonah] said unto them, Take me up, and cast me forth into the sea; so shall the sea be calm unto you: for I know that for my sake this great tempest is upon you" (Jonah 1:12). It worked. With Jonah cast overboard, the storm ceased. Instead of Jonah drowning, the Lord caused a large fish to swallow Jonah whole, and he remained in the creature's belly for three days. Having much time to reflect, he repented of his folly and resolved to do as the Lord commanded. The fish spat him out on dry ground, and Jonah journeyed to Nineveh (see Jonah 2). Let's resume our analysis of Jonah's reactions to life's changes to this point:

- The situation: Jonah flees from his heavenly assignment.
- The change: Jonah is thrown from the ship and swallowed by a fish.
- The reaction: Jonah repents and chooses to follow the Lord's command.

Armed with new determination, Jonah preaches to the disobedient people of Nineveh. "And Jonah began to enter into the city a day's journey, and he cried, and said, Yet forty days, and Nineveh shall be overthrown" (Jonah 3:4). If they did not repent, they'd be destroyed. Remember, Nineveh was an enemy to Israel. Israel's foes had routinely been punished and eliminated by God in the past, and Jonah probably expected the same treatment for the Ninevites. But the opposite happened. The people of Nineveh believed Jonah's words and repented of their sins (see Jonah 3:5–6). The prophesied threat of destruction was averted due to their obedience. One might assume that a prophet would react with happiness at the people's return to righteousness. But Jonah was not happy; he was upset. He had hoped for their destruction and his desires were dashed:

> But it displeased Jonah exceedingly, and he was very angry. And he prayed unto the Lord, and said, I pray thee, O Lord, was not this my saying, when I was yet in my country? Therefore I fled before unto Tarshish: for I knew that thou art a gracious God, and merciful, slow to anger, and of great kindness, and repentest thee of the evil. Therefore now, O Lord, take, I beseech thee, my life from me; for it is better for me to die than to live. (Jonah 4:1–3)

Let's recap Jonah's reactions once more:

- The situation: Jonah preaches annihilation to his enemies at Nineveh.
- The change: The people of Nineveh repent and are spared from destruction.
- The reaction: Jonah gets angry and wishes to die.

The concluding elements of Jonah's story are almost comical, while still eliciting compassion for the rigid-thinking prophet. He makes his way to a hill where he has a view of Nineveh, to "see what would become of the city" (Jonah 4:5). We truly don't know why he was waiting there. We know he was still fuming at the Lord's mercy toward Nineveh. Perhaps Jonah was hopeful the city might yet be destroyed and he could witness it from his hillside perch. The Middle Eastern sun beat down upon Jonah, and the Lord caused a flowering plant to grow and give him shade. Jonah was "exceedingly glad" for the plant (Jonah 4:6). The next day the Lord killed the plant, the sun was as hot as ever, and a brutal wind blew. "And it came to pass, when the sun did arise, that God prepared a vehement east wind; and the sun beat upon the head of Jonah, that he fainted, and wished in himself to die, and said, It is better for me to die than to live" (Jonah 4:8). Let's summarize Jonah's reactions one last time:

- The situation: Jonah gets shade from a plant as he watches Nineveh in the hot sun.
- The change: The plant dies, the wind blows, and Jonah is miserable.
- The reaction: Jonah gets angry and wishes to die.

I feel bad for Jonah. His successful adjustment to change thus far has been limited. He seems pretty miserable. He is so upset that he wants to die. The Lord then teaches him a significant lesson regarding love and charity. He notes how Jonah had more compassion for the shade-giving plant than he did for thousands of God's children. Jonah wept at the death of the plant but had hoped for the destruction of spiritually ignorant men, women, and children. Shouldn't he have had greater compassion for these children of God than he did for a simple plant? Jonah's account ends there, and we are left to wonder regarding his ultimate reaction to the Lord's teachings. But as we look back on Jonah's story, we can find multiple places where he could have adapted more effectively to the changes he experienced. Consider his poor reaction and a hypothetical good reaction that would have reflected emotional resilience:

- Situation #1: Jonah is living comfortably at home.
- Change #1: Jonah is called to leave home and preach to a wicked people.
- What he actually does (poor reaction): Jonah runs away from the assignment.
- What he could have done (emotionally resilient reaction): Jonah could have accepted the assignment and avoided the drama of the ship and the three days inside the fish.

Having reacted more resiliently and obediently to the first change would have surely decreased the type of suffering Jonah experienced due to his noncompliance. Obedience does not necessarily mean we avoid difficulty, but disobedience almost certainly predicts suffering in one form or another. Keeping the commandments does not mean we won't suffer, but it does mean we will be entitled to the Lord's support during such times. In his time at

Nineveh, Jonah could have also avoided some challenges had he adapted more effectively to further unexpected change:

Situation #2: Jonah preaches annihilation to his enemies at Nineveh, expecting their demise.
Change #2: The people of Nineveh repent and are spared from destruction.
What he actually does (poor reaction): Jonah gets angry and wishes to die.
What he could have done (emotionally resilient reaction): Jonah could have sought heavenly counsel and strength, learned to see the people as the Lord saw them, and rejoiced at their redemption.

If Jonah had reacted well to the second change, he could have spared himself the drama of sitting on the hillside and having repeated angry and morbid thoughts. Life seems to have enough difficulty from day to day, such that we should try to avoid behaviors that may create additional challenges. Accepting change can be difficult, but it can create emotional strength, allowing us to cope with future trials.

Let's look at a few roadblocks that inhibit our ability to successfully cope with changes:

Roadblock #1: Thinking We Are Always Correct

In the 1980s sitcom *Happy Days*, Arthur Fonzarelli (known as "the Fonz") was the coolest of the cool. He always had the right comeback and was admired by young and old. However, one of his prominent character flaws was that he was unable to admit he was wrong. Apparently, he was both psychologically *and* physically unable to do it. His resistance to being incorrect was so strong that he couldn't even say the phrase "I was wrong."[43] Sometimes we struggle with having to be right all the time. This can manifest in extreme competitiveness (having to always win), consistent arguing (having to always make a point), and failure to admit guilt (blaming others for negative outcomes). If we believe our every course of action is correct, it becomes very difficult to accept a change of direction. It's fine, and even desirable, to be confident. But there is a difference between being self-assured and refusing to admit you are wrong. In fact, those who cannot admit error usually lack confidence.

---

43 *Happy Days*, created by Gary K. Marshall (Culver City, CA: Miller-Milkis, 1974–81).

Roadblock #2: Poor Self-Concept That Cannot Tolerate Disruption

Building on the previous roadblock, lack of self-confidence can cause challenges with accepting change. Those with poor self-concept often have deep-seated emotional issues that contribute to feelings of incompetence. They experience chronic feelings of doubt, worrying their inadequacies will be exposed. As a result, they compensate by feigning excessive confidence. Such "confidence" is an emotional house of cards; the smallest bump can cause it to shake and fall. I'm reminded of the Savior's analogy in the Sermon on the Mount, wherein he talks of rocky and sandy foundations. Those with houses built on foundations of stone can withstand winds and rains without collapsing. Those with houses built on foundations of sand crumble during turbulence (see Matthew 7:24–27). Emotionally resilient people are truly confident. They chart a course for the future and accept changes as they come. Those without confidence constantly worry that they have made the wrong decision or that an unexpected adjustment will cause their unstable foundation to disintegrate. As such, accepting change is much more threatening to their shaky situation.

Roadblock #3: Lack of Faith in God's Plan for Our Lives

Latter-day Saints should have an advantage over their nonbelieving counterparts simply due to the wealth of knowledge afforded by principles of the restored gospel of Jesus Christ. Not only do we know Heavenly Father is all powerful but also that He constantly supports the righteous. This belief should provide comfort and strength during times of trial, yet transferring that belief from our rational minds to the "fleshy tables of the heart" (2 Corinthians 3:3) can be challenging. Faith seems to be a more emotional than cognitive response. It requires us to believe things that are not necessarily rational or that cannot be experienced by our physical senses. If we truly believe God is at the helm and will direct us for good, then life's changes should be easier to navigate than they often seem to be. Even chronic problems can become more bearable when we know our lives are in line with Father in Heaven's plan. That doesn't mean all questions will be answered and we'll have a clear view of the road ahead; it simply means we'll be able to accept the Lord's will and adapt to changes with confidence. Speaking of the role of faith in an uncertain future, Sharon Eubank, First Counselor in the Relief Society General Presidency, stated, "Take a few more steps on the covenant path, even if it's too dark to see very far. The lights will come back on."44 The stronger our faith in Jesus Christ and in His love for us, the more spiritually self-assured we can become. That assurance can sustain us through unexpected changes in course.

Learning to accept change is a critical life skill because change never stops. That's okay because change is good. It encourages growth. It prevents stagnation. As an example, we used to have a pond in our front yard. It had an electric fountain that circulated the water. As the water gushed from the fountain, the pond remained clean and clear. Then the fountain pump broke, and the water was still. It took me a few weeks to fix it. In that time, the water turned green and was coated with a disgusting film. That same water would have been clear if it had kept moving; it did not become gross until the disruption ceased. Our lives are the same. Although transitions can be hard to accept, and the lure of inactivity seems enticing, change is truly the vehicle to achieve the measure of our existence.

Chapter Nine Exercise

Here is an opportunity for you to examine something specific in your life, to determine possible approaches to help you learn to accept change.

- Think about an unexpected change in your life that happened in the past. Describe it here:

- How did you feel about that change at the time it happened?

---

44 Sharon Eubank, "Christ: The Light That Shines in Darkness," *Ensign*, May 2019, 76.

- Since then, what blessings have you seen in your life because of that change?

- Now think about a potential future change that might happen in your life. Ideally, this should be something nontragic but also something you don't necessarily want to happen. Describe it here:

- How do you think you would feel about this change?

- In what ways could that change be a blessing to you?

Learning to accept and seek change is not only a foundational element of emotional resilience but can also assist in our spiritual progression. This life is a critical step in our journey to become like our Father in Heaven. We truly must "put off the natural man and become a saint" (Mosiah 3:19). That process involves change after change, learning line upon line and precept upon precept. Consider the following scriptures:

> A new heart also will I give you, and a new spirit will I put within you: and I will take away the stony heart out of your flesh, and I will give you an heart of flesh. (Ezekiel 36:26)

> And they all cried with one voice, saying: Yea, we believe all the words which thou hast spoken unto us; and also, we know of their surety and truth, because of the Spirit of the Lord Omnipotent, which has wrought a mighty change in us, or in our hearts, that we have no more disposition to do evil, but to do good continually. (Mosiah 5:2)
>
> Therefore if any man be in Christ, he is a new creature: old things are passed away; behold, all things are become new. (2 Corinthians 5:17)

Each of these scriptures chronicles the transformation from our natural, carnal selves to becoming women and men of Christ. It is often an uncomfortable process. This is by design. If choosing to become like God were easy, then it would be no test of our resolve or determination. Our Father in Heaven wants us to choose Him (see Moses 7:33), but such a choice has little meaning if there are no desirable alternatives. Satan tempts us to pursue a life of ease, taking the low road while resisting the call to grow through change and trial. His lure is very enticing, and his way is initially very pleasant. Yet all who follow his call will eventually experience misery and regret. Our loving Savior beckons us to follow Him, to live the kind of life He lived, and to repent. This purifies our souls and prepares us to ultimately be like Him. President Russell M. Nelson described the pattern of repentance and how it is far more than simply seeking absolution from sin:

> The word for *repentance* in the Greek New Testament is *metanoeo*. The prefix *meta-* means "change." The suffix *-noeo* is related to Greek words that mean "mind," "knowledge," "spirit," and "breath." Thus, when Jesus asks you and me to "repent," He is inviting us to change our mind, our knowledge, our spirit—even the way we breathe. He is asking us to change the way we love, think, serve, spend our time, treat our [spouses], teach our children, and even care for our bodies. Nothing is more liberating, more ennobling, or more crucial to our individual progression than is a regular, daily focus on repentance. Repentance is not an event; it is a process. It is the key to happiness and peace of mind. When coupled with faith, repentance opens our access to the power of the Atonement of Jesus Christ.[45]

---

45 Russell M. Nelson, "We Can Do Better and Be Better," *Ensign*, May 2019, 67.

Changes will come our way; let's acknowledge them and move on. Difficulties will arise; let's engage them and triumph. Some changes will be easier to manage than others. For some individuals who already struggle with chronic physical or mental health issues, new challenges can push them to the breaking point. But never forget the Lord accepts our honest efforts. He will bless us for the good we do, regardless of how small that might seem to us at the time. The overarching process of perfection plays out from moment to moment, change upon change. As we learn to accept and even embrace change as a tool for our growth, we can develop greater emotional strength and ultimately become like our Father in Heaven and our Savior.

Thought Journal

What are two or three things you'd like to remember from this chapter?

Case Study (Accepting Change): "Sylvia"

Sylvia is a nineteen-year-old woman living in the United States. She converted to the gospel of Jesus Christ after being taught by several sets of sister missionaries. Sylvia developed a great fondness for the missionaries who taught her and immediately knew she would serve a mission when the time came. When she got her patriarchal blessing, she received many promises that referred to her future missionary efforts. Upon turning nineteen, she submitted her mission papers. She dreamed of going to an undeveloped foreign country, feeling she could make a difference among the people there. Her mission call arrived, and she had been assigned to labor in the Accra Ghana Mission. She was thrilled.

Her departure date was in six months, and she began preparing right away. She learned everything she could about the culture. She started experimenting with their cooking styles and becoming familiar with their customs. When she was about one month from entering the missionary training center, the COVID-19 pandemic covered the earth. Within weeks, almost all US missionaries serving on foreign soil had been reassigned to domestic missions. Sylvia worried she would not be able to go to Ghana but trusted that the Lord would send her where she had been assigned. She believed the prophets received revelation when making such assignments and had further received a spiritual witness that her assignment was correct.

In the coming weeks, Sylvia received an email that she was being reassigned to a mission in Southern California. It was practically the opposite of what she had hoped for. It was an affluent area with many creature comforts. She felt the work would be more difficult and she would not be able to make as significant an impact as she could have with the African people. Sylvia was upset. Why would this happen? If she was supposed to go to Africa in the first place, why wouldn't the Lord make it so? Couldn't He just end the pandemic so she could serve in the location she was supposed to serve in? Sylvia started to wonder if her capacity for revelation was off or if she should even serve a mission at all.

Review the three roadblocks previously discussed in this chapter (Thinking We Are Always Correct, Poor Self-Concept That Cannot Tolerate Disruption, Lack of Faith in God's Plan for Our Lives).

- In your opinion, which of these roadblocks is preventing Sylvia from moving forward? It could be one or more.

- Describe how each roadblock you have identified prevents Sylvia from progressing.

- Based on what you've learned in this chapter, what would be a helpful strategy (or strategies) for Sylvia to consider?

Resolution

Sylvia talked with her bishop and with her best friend. She read many conference talks that helped her feel peace despite her difficult situation. She prayed diligently to understand the Lord's will regarding her mission assignment. Sylvia still had not received an answer to her prayers when the time came to begin her missionary training. She continued to seek answers through study. She departed for the Southern California mission field, still wondering if she was in the right place. Through ongoing study, prayer, and fasting, Sylvia eventually achieved a peaceful feeling about her changed mission assignment. She decided to serve the Lord no matter where she was, understanding that her call to be a missionary was more critical than her place of service.

Please see Appendix I for additional exercises for Chapter Nine.

CHAPTER TEN
EMOTIONAL RESILIENCE ELEMENT #6:
BUILDING SECURE RELATIONSHIPS

ESTABLISHING RELATIONSHIPS IS CRITICAL TO our progression. Generally speaking, human beings are social creatures. I believe we enjoyed loving relationships prior to coming to Earth, and Joseph Smith taught that social interactions continue beyond the grave (see D&C 130:2). The sequence of the earth's creation underscored the value of human connection. After Adam was formed, and before the creative work was considered complete, Heavenly Father ensured Adam was not left to himself. "And the Lord God said, It is not good that the man should be alone; I will make him an help meet for him" (Genesis 2:18). Eve was created. Thus began the mortal version of relationships, along with their potential for happiness, frustration, support, betrayal, love, hate, and everything else associated with the extremely complicated process of learning to get along with others. Relationships are an essential part of our lives and can help improve our mental health. In fact, the lack of social connectedness can be considered pathological in certain cases.[46]

Harry Harlow was an American psychologist who investigated the function and necessity of human connection. In the 1950s many researchers presumed that human relationships were mostly for practical utility. They figured children needed parents for crucial things like food, clothing, and shelter, but emotional support was not essential. It was reasoned that one could literally die from not eating, but if one did not have the experience of being loved and cared for, that would only be a minor inconvenience. One of the scientific challenges of that time was the assumption behind the prevailing psychological models. Behaviorism was cutting-edge knowledge and presumed one could only study that which could be objectively observed and measured. Regarding parenting, you could measure the amount of food or clothing a parent gave to a child, but

---

[46] *Diagnostic and Statistical Manual of Mental Disorders: DSM-5.* 5th ed. (Arlington, VA: American Psychiatric Association, 2013), 652–55, 672–75.

how could you measure the amount of love or concern one felt for another? Such intangible expressions were unscientific to behavioral psychologists and were not typically investigated.[47]

Still, Harlow wondered if there was more to human relationships than simply practical interactions. He tested his theories on rhesus monkeys, an experimental design that would never be condoned by contemporary psychology ethics boards. However, in the 1950s and '60s, this was a common practice that helped researchers discover valuable information. Harlow separated infant monkeys from their mothers upon birth, constructing two surrogate devices to provide essential care. Both of the devices had a feeding nipple that provided nourishment. They were the approximate size of a grown rhesus female monkey and had a heating system, making them warm to the touch. Both surrogates were made of wire mesh. One was only the exposed wire structure, while the other was covered with a soft terry cloth. Both devices were warm and provided adequate sustenance, but one was pleasant to the touch while the other was less so. Previous experiments had shown the infant monkeys had a preference for soft items such as cloth diapers, so the researchers wondered if the surrogate covered in terrycloth would be more desirable than the other. The results were fascinating.[48]

In certain trials, the cloth surrogate provided milk and the wire surrogate did not. In this case, the monkeys spent many more hours with their "cloth mothers" than with the "wire mothers." This seemed reasonable, as the monkeys would naturally prefer the unit that could provide them with needed food. However, in other trials, the conditions were reversed. The wire surrogate provided milk and the cloth mother did not. One might assume the monkeys would spend more time with their wire mothers in this case, due to the availability of milk. But the opposite occurred. The monkeys spent far more time with their cloth mothers than with the wire mothers. In many cases, the monkeys would simply cling to the cloth mothers, despite the fact they received no physical sustenance. The researchers began to understand there was more to the primates' needs than simple feeding. Subsequent experiments had infant monkeys explore a foreign environment that contained fearful stimuli. If there was a cloth mother in the room, the monkeys explored their surroundings more confidently. When frightened, they returned to their "mother" and sought comfort. When the cloth mother

---

[47] Kendra Cherry, "Harry Harlow and the Nature of Affection," *Verywell Mind*, December 3, 2020, verywellmind.com/harry-harlow-and-the-nature-of-love-2795255. Accessed December 4, 2020.
[48] Harry F. Harlow, "The Nature of Love," *American Psychologist*, December 1958, 673–85.

was absent, the monkeys showed less courage and even retreated to a fetal position when scared.[49]

The results of these studies confirm what modern-day common sense suggests to all: relationships are important. They provide more than just meeting basic physical needs. They have the capacity to furnish feelings of belonging, safety, understanding, and love. Building secure relationships is a key component of emotional resilience. Even to the layperson, it makes good sense. Supportive connections help us respond better to difficulties and endure trials with strength. As a personal example, I left home for Brigham Young University when I was eighteen. I am the oldest of eight children and definitely a homebody. I had been away from home a week at a time for backpacking and camping trips but otherwise had spent my entire life with my parents and siblings. Going to college was my first significant away-from-home experience. After getting settled in Provo, I remember my family dropping me off at the Maeser building for some orientation meeting. As we parted ways, I watched our blue van drive off. I was overwhelmed with fear and uncertainty. I didn't know anyone at school and was terrified to be on my own. I sat on the stone steps of the building, gently weeping. A kindhearted professor asked if he could help, and we went into the orientation together. For the next few days I had difficulty holding back tears, as I felt alone and was quite homesick.

This was long before the days of cell phones and the internet. Long-distance telephone calls were expensive. Affordable communication consisted of mailing a letter. Not only was I away from my family and friends but I also knew it would probably be a long time before I was able to talk with or see them again. But there was one exception. I had a friend from home who was headed to BYU as well. We had become close, and I eagerly awaited her arrival. When she came, I helped her move in and subsequently spent much time at her apartment. After that, my emotional experience changed dramatically. Although I didn't spend all my time with her, knowing she was there for support was all my heart required to settle down. I was like the infant monkey exploring my new surroundings, feeling more confident because I knew that comfort and safety were not far away. My ability to cope with the stress of being away from home and in a strange setting was fortified by a solid relationship. This is the effect of secure relationships on emotional resilience.

Building secure relationships takes substantial time and effort. They are living entities that require appropriate nourishment to survive. Feeding

---

49 Harlow, "The Nature of Love," 673–85.

relationships helps them grow stronger; neglecting them causes them to falter. Some believe that if they don't intentionally damage relationships, the relationships will remain the same and not worsen. This is not true. Most things, if not cared for, will deteriorate over time. Take our backyard fence, for example. We've lived in our current home for about fifteen years, and the fence was built a quarter of a century ago. I've never done anything to damage my fence, yet some of the boards are rotting. I've had to reinforce certain portions, and soon I'll need to replace the entire structure. Even though I've never intentionally harmed my fence, it has fallen into disrepair. In addition, I've never been at odds with my fence. I've never wished for it to fall down or deliberately neglected it. Quite frankly, in the fifteen years we've lived here, I haven't given it much thought. That is precisely the problem. Had I been more diligent, focusing on weak spots and making repairs along the way, my fence would be in much better shape. The deterioration of relationships can happen through active injury *or* passive neglect. Relationships remain resilient when they are regularly mended, rebuilt, and strengthened.

One of the most significant predictors of secure relationships is a healthy sense of emotional intimacy. Emotional intimacy is the ability to be close to and vulnerable with another person. Most everyone yearns for deep, satisfying connective bonds with others, but these can be difficult to achieve. Those who have experienced significant betrayal can find this particularly challenging. We are born with natural trust. Infants bond with those who meet their physical and emotional needs. Children are innocent and typically follow adults with few questions. As youth, we enter relationships with optimism. Then the first betrayal happens. Someone falls through with a commitment. Another intentionally deceives us. In the worst cases, people we have welcomed into the inner sanctums of our hearts cause destruction through selfish and insensitive behavior. We are no longer the trusting children of yesteryear and instead build stone walls around our hearts to keep them constantly guarded against another potential betrayal. While this may keep us safe, it also keeps us stagnant. Developing emotional intimacy requires us to break down the walls and let people in. For some, this can be a painstaking process that requires years. Yet it is worth the effort, as having strong, secure relationships becomes a meaningful foundation to help us get through difficult times.

Not only do we need supportive earthly relationships but we also need supportive heavenly relationships as well. Contrary to our relationships with fellow mortals, we are completely in control of the quality of our relationship with Heavenly Father and Jesus Christ. They will never betray us. They will never fall through on a commitment. They will never ignore our call. The Savior said, "Behold, I stand at the door, and knock: if any man hear my voice, and open the door, I will come in to him, and will sup with him, and he with me" (Revelation 3:20). They are ever ready to have an amazing relationship with us; we just have to make the first move and open the door. I've often pondered if one of Father in Heaven's greatest griefs is how so many of His children have essentially forgotten Him. I believe many of us enjoyed a wonderful relationship with Him before coming to Earth. As we embarked on our mortal journey, I wonder if He gently and sincerely asked us to stay in close contact. Perhaps that way we could continue to experience the same sort of relationship we had developed with Him to that point. Maybe we said, "Of course! I'll pray every day. I'll stay close to the Spirit. I'll never do anything to damage my relationship with You." I wonder if He smiled and hugged us one last time before we left, knowing very well that the veil of mortality would soon obscure our remembrance so that only He would recall that last heavenly interaction. We arrived on Earth, and soon enough, God, our loving confidant, became no more than a stranger to so many of us. I wonder if that is one of His utmost sorrows—that we don't have the same relationship with Him as we did before. I believe He yearns for us to rekindle that association. We should seek for the same thing. Building, or in the truest sense, rebuilding our relationship with Heavenly Father and Jesus Christ will provide bedrock foundations for us to successfully endure any challenge we face (see Helaman 5:12).

Let's consider some roadblocks that impact our capacity to build secure relationships, both earthly and heavenly.

Roadblock #1: Not Loving One Another

On the surface this seems simple, as one might say, "Of course I understand that I need to love those I want to have good relationships with." Although true, this process is more nuanced than one might expect. In the Sermon on the Mount, Jesus taught that the old law instructed people to love their neighbors and hate their enemies. He gave them new doctrine, commanding them to love their enemies as well (see Matthew 5:43–44). Too often, we embrace the old law instead of the new. I have noticed, often on social media, that people are willing to unleash extremely hateful statements toward groups or individuals. This frequently happens in a political context but is not limited to that. In the same breath, we plead for an end to violence and bigotry. I don't think we can be hateful in one instance and then expect peace in the next. I have come to believe that unless we are willing to eliminate all hate from our own hearts, regardless of the target or whether we feel the person deserves it, we are part of the problem. If we reserve a portion of our soul to harbor hatred, our ability to form secure relationships will be forever stunted. Loving one another as the Savior commanded includes loving all, regardless of political belief, religious affiliation, or behavioral choices. As we purge hate from our lives, we expand our capacity for solid relationships.

Roadblock #2: Waiting for Others to Make the First Move

Creating a solid relationship involves emotional risk. Returning to the concept of emotional intimacy, one of the reasons we tend to be emotionally guarded is because we have been hurt in the past. I don't believe anyone is immune from this experience. Everyone, to one degree or another, has some hesitation to lower their guard, allow someone in, and risk getting wounded. This creates a potential problem, almost like an emotional standoff. Both individuals wait for the other to drop their defenses before they drop their own. This can lead to months or years of barriers remaining firmly in place, keeping the relationship stagnant. If you want to strengthen your relationships, you need to make the first move. You need to be the one to lower your shield and put down your sword, signaling to the other that it is okay for them to do so as well. In many cases, the other individual will follow suit, creating fertile soil for emotional intimacy to grow. Being the first to act involves risk, but there is no effective way to improve a relationship without taking this gamble. Establishing secure relationships means moving forward confidently and showing others that you are willing to be vulnerable.

Roadblock #3: Misunderstanding the Character of Deity

When I was thirteen, a new family moved into our ward. They had a son who was close to my age. That was our only similarity. We didn't get along well. In fact, we quickly became enemies. I knew very little about him but had already formed a hasty and inaccurate opinion of his character. In time, as we got to know each other better, we realized we had many things in common. Ultimately, he became one of my best friends, but not until I invested the energy to truly come to know him. We are unlikely to draw close to people we view as hostile, distant, or overly judgmental. What happens to our relationship with Heavenly Father if we view Him that way? Some feel that God is always disappointed in them. Others feel like He is constantly waiting to punish them if He can catch them in an act of disobedience. Still others believe He is aloof, casually watching our lives but making little effort to get involved. All of these ideas are fallacies. One of Satan's greatest deceptions has been to distort our understanding of Heavenly Father's character. By casting Him in unflattering hues, Satan discourages our desire to grow close to our Heavenly Father. As we better understand the true nature of our Father in Heaven, we discover that He is loving, patient, and infinitely kind. This facilitates our efforts to form a secure relationship with Him and His Son.

Building solid relationships may seem counterintuitive to emotional resilience. One may say, "I thought being emotionally resilient meant being able to handle things on your own." That is not what emotional resilience means. It means being able to withstand stress and grow from difficulty, using *all available resources* at your disposal. Some of these resources will be internal, such as personal competency or tenacity. Other resources will be external, including having supportive friends and a strong relationship with the Savior. At times we believe that going it alone is a mark of advanced fortitude. I disagree. There is nothing bold about refusing aid or never reaching out for assistance. In fact, it takes much greater courage to humbly reach out for help and admit your individual efforts are insufficient to the task. Strong relationships add multiple resources to our emotional armory, making us better prepared to endure challenges.

Chapter Ten Exercise

Here is an opportunity for you to examine something specific in your life, to determine possible approaches to help you build secure relationships.

- Think about one of your most important relationships. Briefly describe the individual and what you like about the relationship.

- Consider *one aspect* of that relationship that you'd like to see improve. Describe that aspect here.

- Overall, what do you need to do to improve that aspect of your relationship?

- What is something you can do *today* to improve that aspect of your relationship?

Forming solid mortal relationships is very helpful in increasing emotional resilience. Forming solid relationships with God is *essential* to our progression. I suppose we could possibly make it through life without significant help from other people. It would be an unpleasant struggle, and we would certainly not thrive. However, it is completely impossible to meet the measure of our creation, becoming like our Heavenly Father, without developing a strong relationship with Him.

In the grand Intercessory Prayer, the Savior prays for His Apostles. Can you imagine this? To hear the Lord Jesus Christ pray for you specifically? I'm certain the Apostles were overcome with emotion, similar to the Nephites who had a comparable experience: "And no one can conceive of the joy which filled our souls at the time we heard him pray for us unto the Father" (3 Nephi 17:17). As Jesus prayed for His beloved associates, He made a notable statement: "And this is life eternal, that they might know thee the only true God, and Jesus Christ, whom thou hast sent" (John 17:3). When Jesus invites us to "know" God and Himself, I believe He means more than just knowing They exist or knowing Their characteristics. I think He means we need to know Them like we know a close friend. We need to develop a relationship with Them that is more than superficial. This involves work on our part. But remember, this process is simply a renewing of a relationship instead of forging a new one. Our Father in Heaven has not forgotten our previous premortal associations; we are the ones who cannot recall. President Brigham Young commented on the joyous reunion we will have upon reuniting with our beloved Heavenly Father:

> When you are prepared to see our Father, you will see a being with whom you have long been acquainted, and He will receive you into His arms, and you will be ready to fall into His embrace and kiss Him . . . you will be so glad and joyful.[50]

Rekindling our relationship with God involves learning about Him through study. Our Savior condescended to live among us so we could have a firsthand account of His magnificent characteristics. He is the exact similitude of the Father in every way, so to know one is to know the other. Prayer is an amazing tool to become better acquainted with God. I've wondered why we are commanded to pray, basically recounting to the Father those things that He already knows. When I report my day to Him, there are no surprises. He watched my every move with rapt attention. He commands us to pray not for His benefit but for ours. It is a humbling and potentially beautiful experience. We become vulnerable, laying down our pretense and baring our souls. Just as the practice of vulnerability helps us develop greater emotional intimacy with mortals, it helps us develop greater emotional intimacy with God. As our relationship with God strengthens, we learn there is no trial or challenge we cannot overcome with His help. We become like Nephi:

> And it came to pass that I, Nephi, said unto my father: I will go and do the things which the Lord hath commanded, for I know that the Lord giveth no commandments unto the children of men, save he shall prepare a way for them that they may accomplish the thing which he commandeth them. (1 Nephi 3:7)

---

50 Brigham Young, in *Journal of Discourses*, 4:54–55.

Or Shadrach, Meshach, and Abednego:

> If it be so, our God whom we serve is able to deliver us from the burning fiery furnace, and he will deliver us out of thine hand, O king. But if not, be it known unto thee, O king, that we will not serve thy gods, nor worship the golden image which thou hast set up. (Daniel 3:17–18)

Or Joseph Smith:

> Therefore, dearly beloved brethren, let us cheerfully do all things that lie in our power; and then may we stand still, with the utmost assurance, to see the salvation of God, and for his arm to be revealed. (D&C 123:17)

Learning to rely on others, including our Heavenly Father and Jesus Christ, will greatly enhance our capacity to survive and thrive through challenges. When we take our own strength, add the strength of others, and combine that with the limitless powers of heaven, there is no challenge we cannot overcome. Do what is necessary in your life to increase the quality of and potential for these relationships.

Thought Journal

What are two or three things you'd like to remember from this chapter?

Case Study (Building Secure Relationships): "Daniel"

Daniel is a thirty-five-year-old man. He has been married for five years. Contrary to most of his Latter-day Saint peers, Daniel married at an older age. He served a full-time mission and then was single for ten years until he finally met his wife. Although the two of them are happily married, Daniel's dating experiences prior to marriage were difficult. He has always struggled with self-confidence. For a period of time, those feelings increased to the point of depression. Daniel worked with a counselor for a few months and was able to resolve some of his doubts, but he never developed a strong sense of self or a solid degree of self-assurance. He has always worried that he is letting others down and is quick to blame himself when something goes wrong. His lack of confidence made dating a challenge, as he constantly stressed that he would not be accepted by others.

When Daniel met his wife, Melissa, he was instantly attracted to her. She was beautiful to him, both inside and out. He felt completely unworthy of her companionship, always comparing her strengths with his weaknesses. Nevertheless, they developed a friendship that ultimately blossomed into marriage. Like many young marriages, their relationship lacked the emotional depth that can only be achieved through years of companionship and effort. Even though they have now been married for five years, their relationship is still somewhat superficial. Daniel loves Melissa very much and is sincerely committed to her, yet he is hesitant to try to deepen their relationship, as he fears she may reject him if he expresses his vulnerability.

For a couple of years, Daniel has had spiritual impressions that he needs to improve his relationship with Melissa. He has felt they need to become more emotionally bonded and start discussing deeper, more substantial issues. However, he is afraid of moving forward. In his rational thoughts, Daniel recognizes that Melissa loves him and is very unlikely to reject him. He is convinced of her love for him. Yet, in his emotional thoughts, he fears opening up emotionally and getting hurt. He has dropped hints about the need for greater emotional connectedness in the marriage, hoping Melissa would initiate a conversation about this, but nothing has happened. The spiritual impressions toward action have not decreased, and Daniel finds himself stuck between what he feels he should do and his fears of moving forward.

Review the three roadblocks previously discussed in this chapter (Not Loving One Another, Waiting for Others to Make the First Move, Misunderstanding the Character of Deity).

- In your opinion, which of these roadblocks is preventing Daniel from moving forward? It could be one or more.

- Describe how each roadblock you have identified prevents Daniel from progressing.

- Based on what you've learned in this chapter, what would be a helpful strategy (or strategies) for Daniel to consider?

Resolution

Daniel decided to fast and pray about his problem. In time he received a prompting to review his patriarchal blessing, something he had not done for a while. As he studied the blessing, he was impressed with two themes: the Lord expected him to act, and He would support Daniel in his righteous endeavors. Daniel resolved to find a time to talk with Melissa and express his fears. As they discussed the issues, he was surprised to discover that Melissa had been having similar feelings. She had been impressed that she should be extra kind to Daniel and help him feel loved and supported. They determined that they would devote some time, on a weekly basis, to sit and openly discuss any problems or other concerns they had in their marriage.

Please see Appendix J for additional exercises for Chapter Ten.

CHAPTER ELEVEN
EMOTIONAL RESILIENCE ELEMENT #7: SENSE OF CONTROL

IN 1971 PSYCHOLOGY PROFESSOR PHILIP Zimbardo conducted a social psychological experiment that has become internationally famous. He investigated the concept of power, particularly what would happen when one group of people felt they had power over another group. Zimbardo recruited college students at Stanford University to participate in a two-week experience in which half of them would be "guards" and the other half "inmates" in a simulated prison environment. The students were randomly assigned to their roles. The guards were outfitted in uniforms and given nightsticks but were instructed to inflict no physical harm on the inmates. They were further instructed, in a vague manner, to do what was needed to manage the prisoners. Those who had been assigned as inmates were actually arrested in their homes by local law enforcement and transported to the prison site. After arriving, they were stripped and had to stand naked for a time. Eventually they received their wardrobe and were taken to their cells. Inmates were kept in their cells for long periods, had a work assignment, and were afforded three meals plus three supervised bathroom trips per day.[51]

The environment quickly devolved, as if the participants completely forgot that just days before they were fellow university students. The guards became more aggressive and dehumanizing toward the inmates. They asserted significant control, barking out commands and referring to inmates in impersonal terms. While physical violence was prohibited, verbal violence became one of the most common forms of interaction between prisoners and guards. All participants had been prescreened and determined not to have serious psychological problems. Even so, five of the prisoners had to be released early for showing symptoms of "extreme emotional depression, crying, rage, and acute anxiety." Although the

---
51 Craig Haney, Curtis Banks, and Philip Zimbardo, "A Study of Prisoners and Guards in a Simulated Prison," *Naval Research Reviews*, September 1973, 1–17.

experiment was intended to last for two weeks, it was terminated after only six days because of the considerable effect it had on both guards and prisoners. They had assumed their roles so completely that fantasy had become reality, yielding bona fide emotional responses.[52] Such an experiment would never be approved by today's ethics boards. Some have criticized Zimbardo's methodology as unscientific.[53] Even so, the reported reactions of the participants were genuine and provided valuable insight into the concept of perceived power.

In post-experiment interviews, Zimbardo reported that the prisoners were troubled by the fact that they had no control over their circumstances. No matter what they did, they seemed to get a negative response. As the guards exercised more and more control over them, the prisoners quickly learned their behavior had no effect on outcomes. Being treated like prisoners, they started to act like prisoners. Regarding this, the researchers stated,

> As the environment became more unpredictable, and previously learned assumptions about a just and orderly world were no longer functional, prisoners ceased to initiate any action. They moved about on orders and when in their cells rarely engaged in any purposeful activity. . . . Since their behavior did not seem to have any contingent relationship to environmental consequences, the prisoners essentially gave up and stopped behaving.[54]

Having a healthy sense of control is an essential element of emotional resilience. Consider its utility in stressful situations. Sometimes we make plans but something goes wrong. Those who feel they have control over their lives can adjust and move forward. Those who believe they have no control feel like victims to their circumstances. Yet in the Lord's plan, we were never intended to feel like victims. Our Father in Heaven has blessed us with the capacity to take control of our lives, through the wonderful gift of agency. At the same time, He expects us to rely heavily upon Him for direction. To use a common analogy, it's like driving a car. We are the drivers and are tasked with moving forward. But Father in Heaven is the navigator. We operate the vehicle but follow His directions on where to go. As agents unto ourselves, we make our own choices but wisely follow counsel and act when commanded by God.

---

52 Haney, Banks, and Zimbardo, "A Study of Prisoners and Guards," 1–17.
53 Thibault Le Texier, "Debunking the Stanford Prison Experiment," *American Psychologist*, October 2019, 823–39.
54 Haney, Banks, and Zimbardo, "A Study of Prisoners and Guards," 16.

Agency, sometimes referred to as moral agency, is a bedrock principle of mortality. It was one of the main points of contention in the war in heaven. Lucifer wanted to suspend agency in favor of saving all Heavenly Father's children. Heavenly Father knew agency was so critical to our progression that He permitted Satan's rebellion and lost many of His children forever. Agency is both the power and the obligation to choose. Sometimes we view this concept mostly in terms of the former: we know it gives us the power to make choices. But what of the obligation? Does righteous exercise of our agency include putting it on the shelf, letting our circumstances dictate our course? I don't believe so. Satan has been at war with agency since his initial insurgence. He was not able to erase it completely but has not ceased his efforts. Now his attack is fought one person at a time. He wants us to *choose* to limit our agency, either through sin, passivity, fear, or other situations that create either real or perceived obstacles to progress. In some ways, understanding the value and purpose of agency may be one of the most significant concepts of emotional resilience. Everything begins with our choices. If we choose poorly, or choose *not* to choose, we become observers instead of actors. Elder D. Todd Christofferson of the Quorum of the Twelve Apostles taught,

> In years past we generally used the term *free agency*. That is not incorrect. More recently we have taken note that *free agency* does not appear in the scriptures. . . . But the word *agency* appears either by itself or with the modifier *moral*: "That every man may act in doctrine and principle . . . according to the *moral agency* which I have given unto him, that every man may be accountable for his own sins in the day of judgment" (D&C 101:78; emphasis added). When we use the term *moral agency*, we are appropriately emphasizing the accountability that is an essential part of the divine gift of agency. We are moral beings and agents unto ourselves, free to choose but also responsible for our choices.[55]

Lehi taught his son Jacob that God divided His creations into two categories: things to act and things to be acted upon. He further taught, "The Lord God gave unto man that he should act for himself" (2 Nephi 2:16). As human beings, we are in the category of "things to act." Yet, through our

---
55 D. Todd Christofferson, "Moral Agency," *Ensign*, June 2009, 47.

choices, we sometimes find ourselves in the category of "things to be acted upon." Let me provide some examples.

In my professional career, I've worked with many individuals who have committed serious crimes. I've visited with them in jails and prisons. I've counseled them while they've been on probation and parole. One memorable visit happened when I had to travel to Walla Walla State Penitentiary—Washington's most secure prison that houses their most dangerous criminals—to evaluate an inmate. In order to gain access to my client, I had to pass a background check, have my possessions searched, and go through about eight controlled doorways. As I noted my surroundings, I marveled at how securely monitored this facility was. There were cameras everywhere and guards on patrol. Because of his previous choices, my client had largely become a person to be acted upon. When our meeting was over, I passed through each checkpoint and out the prison doors. Despite an intense desire to leave as well, my client had no such option.

To use a more germane example, many years ago I sustained a debilitating back injury. I hurt myself trying to lift an item that was far too heavy. But the trauma wasn't just due to the heavy object. I was also out of shape. At the time I was overweight, and my core muscles were weak. I hadn't always been that way; in former times, I was in great physical condition. During such times I could easily have lifted the item that did me in. My choices to eat poorly and not exercise made me weak. My choice to lift the heavy item by myself resulted in injury. After the accident, I could barely walk. I couldn't bend at the waist without serious pain. I couldn't tie my shoes. I was truly being acted upon, and it was miserable. My recovery took months, and even today I must be careful about what and how I lift things. As I have reflected on that time in my life, the choice to lift the heavy object was not the only problem. It was just the last piece of a larger problem I had been creating for years through laziness and inactivity. I hadn't actively tried to get in bad shape. But it was the lack of choice—the lack of drive to eat healthy and exercise regularly—that ultimately led to my being acted upon by pain and discomfort for several months. Agency is not simply about avoiding sin. It is also about actively choosing good things that will keep us physically and emotionally capable, thus preserving our ability to be actors.

Sometimes we find ourselves in situations where we have no external control, due to no fault of our own. While we may not always be able to control the outward events of our lives, we can almost always control our internal experience through practice and discipline. Developing an appropriate sense of control involves understanding the concepts of internal versus external locus of control.

An internal locus of control is when we believe that our choices influence our outcomes. An external locus of control is when we feel controlled by outside forces more often than not. For example, suppose a student writes a research paper and earns an A. An internal locus of control would say, "I worked really hard and studied diligently. I got the A because I put in the effort." An external locus of control would say, "The teacher must have been in a good mood when she graded the paper. It was an easy assignment, and everyone probably got A's." Can you see the difference? When we have an internal locus of control, we credit ourselves for work and effort. This can build confidence and resilience. When problems arise, those with an internal locus will say, "I've gotten through problems before by doing my part; I can do it again." An external locus attributes success to outside forces such as fortuity or dumb luck. When problems arise, those with an external locus will say, "Who knows how this will turn out? Perhaps I'll succeed, and perhaps I won't; it just depends on who or what is in charge." This locus naturally leads to lack of confidence and feelings of powerlessness. Both loci tend to have a compounding effect: the more we use them, the stronger they become in our lives. It's like an upward or downward spiral, leading either to greater strength or increased helplessness.

Having a proper balance of these loci is critical. Satan tries to tempt us on either side of the equation. On the one hand, he'll say, "There's nothing you can do. No matter what you try, you won't be able to succeed. You may as well just give up now." These lies can lead us to feel worthless and powerless. Whether these thoughts come from Satan, mental illness, or from our own distorted thinking, they remain untrue. Our ability to act remains intact, but it is effectively inert if we choose to do nothing. On the other hand, Satan will say, "You don't need any help. You can do it all on your own. Don't bother others for assistance." On the surface these seem like positive and helpful statements, but they are devilishly deceptive. Humility is critical in our spiritual development. We need to recognize that despite our best efforts, we were never intended to make it through life without the help of others or our Father in Heaven. Developing a healthy sense of control involves the righteous and intentional exercise of our agency, while at the same time understanding that accepting earthly and heavenly help from others is essential.

Let's talk about some roadblocks that can impact our sense of control.

Roadblock #1: Seeing Ourselves as Objects Instead of Actors

When it comes to a sense of control, perception is crucial. In my psychology career, I've worked with thousands of individuals who are emotionally stuck. Sometimes, they have not made substantial progress in years. In many of these cases, they cite a significant event in their past that stopped their growth. Most of the time, the referenced event was truly meaningful and debilitating. As a result, such events continue to hold significant power over certain clients. In almost every case, the event is long past, yet the people involved continue to be held emotionally hostage by their past, feeling as if they cannot move forward because of something that happened years or even decades ago. I understand and empathize with those who have experienced such devastation caused by events beyond their control. But these clients will remain stuck until they view themselves as actors and not objects. To be sure, working through past trauma can take a considerable amount of time and effort and is by no means an easy process. However, it begins by taking control where this can be done. Instead of surrendering our agency to past events, we need to look at potential ways forward and do what we can with our current abilities. The past is only as influential as we permit it to be in the present. We have control over our perceptions. As we align our thoughts and beliefs with truth, we will experience a greater sense of healthy control.

Roadblock #2: Lack of Confidence in Our Abilities

Appropriate confidence is essential in developing a sense of control. If you believe you can do something, you may still fail. Even though belief alone is insufficient to achieve all tasks, it gets us on the path to potential success. If you believe you *cannot* do something, you will almost always fail. The odds of success may be the same for those who believe in themselves and those who don't. But those who lack confidence are much less likely to even try. If one does not try, failure is guaranteed. The Soviet Union and the United States of America inaugurated the space race in the mid-1950s. For the first time in history, humans developed technologies to leave the planet and explore outer space. Space travel was the purview of well-funded government agencies such as NASA for decades. No one but the government was building spaceships. Then some started to wonder, "Could I do that too?" In the early 2000s private agencies began developing technologies for space travel. One of the most notable of these is SpaceX, which has pioneered many advances in human spaceflight. If its founder, Elon Musk, would have said, "There's no way I can build a spaceship," then despite his intellect and vast financial resources, we would not have SpaceX today. Having confidence in our abilities is very important in developing a proper sense of control.

Roadblock #3: Misunderstanding the Concept of Grace

Latter-day Saints enjoy a robust understanding of the doctrine of grace, yet the subtleties of this doctrine can be difficult to understand. The prophet Nephi taught, "We know that it is by grace that we are saved, after all we can do" (2 Nephi 25:23). Our own efforts alone are insufficient to save us, but they are critical in the process. We must take responsibility for our own progression, making good choices and keeping our covenants. Not only does this qualify us for the Savior's redeeming power but it also prepares us for life with our Father in Heaven and helps us develop His characteristics. The idea of "I'll just do the bare minimum because Jesus saves me anyway" can lead to less joy and progress in this life. The Lord expects far more than the bare minimum from His children. If we want to become like Him, the bare minimum will not suffice. We need to take control of our lives and strive every day to improve. As we do so, our efforts will be consecrated and eventually perfected through the Savior's Atonement. Bonnie L. Oscarson, former Young Women General President, taught,

> We all need to seek to have our hearts and very natures changed so that we no longer have a desire to follow the ways of the world but to please God. True conversion is a process that takes place over a period of time and involves a willingness to exercise faith.[56]

In terms of our eternal progression, we are required to do our part: no more, no less. What exactly constitutes our part? In my experience, it's a moving target. Each day it could mean something different; some days require significant effort and other days not as much. That's one of the reasons it is essential to have the influence of the Holy Ghost in our lives. Every day, He can guide us to know what our portion is and what we need to leave to the Lord. When we have a healthy sense of control, we see problems as manageable. Much of this perception comes from past successes. As we reflect

---

56 Bonnie L. Oscarson, "Do I Believe?" *Ensign*, May 2016, 88.

on prior difficulties and see what we were able to do to overcome them, we build confidence for the next challenge.

CHAPTER ELEVEN EXERCISE

Here is an opportunity for you to examine something specific in your life, to determine possible approaches to help you increase a healthy sense of control.

- Think about a recent accomplishment you achieved. Describe it here.

- List five things that contributed to the achievement of that event; label them as "internal" (things you did) or "external" (things others did or situational influences).

- Of the five contributing factors, how many were internal? How many were external?

- If you have more external factors than internal factors, try to come up with more internal factors so they exceed the number of external factors. Write them here:

There is an old English fable regarding a farmer who wanted to hire a helper for his farm. As he interviewed potential prospects, each told of their skill in farming and their diligent work ethic. One interviewee caught his attention. When the farmer asked him why he was qualified for the position, the young man simply said, "I can sleep while the wind blows." It was an oddly confident answer, and without really knowing why, the farmer hired this youth. The farmer's instinct proved accurate, as the farmhand was a good worker. One dark night, the farmer awoke with a start. A severe wind was blowing, meaning his property and animals were in potential danger. He went to alert the young worker, but the boy was sleeping peacefully. Somewhat perturbed but at the same time recalling the youth's claim that he could "sleep while the wind blows," the farmer put on his coat and ran to the barn. Expecting the worst, he imagined the barn blown over and the cows exposed to the harsh elements. But as he entered the barn, the cows were peacefully content. He noticed how the farmhand had repaired the barn slats and secured the doors; all inside were secure. Next the farmer worried about his haystacks, fearing they were blowing away. But he found them all tightly secured with ropes, easily withstanding the gale. Realizing his property was safe, the farmer returned to his home. Once again, he noticed the farmhand in peaceful slumber. He now knew what the boy meant when he said he could "sleep while the wind blows."[57] The farmhand's confidence and peace of mind came from his diligent effort. Instead of waiting for disaster to strike and dealing with the aftermath, he exercised his agency and prepared beforehand.

Establishing a sense of control in our lives involves taking action when we can. Many, many circumstances are partially or completely out of our control. Instead of focusing on what we are unable to do, we should focus on what we *can* do and then act. Consider the example of the prodigal son. His father, and I presume his mother as well, were likely devastated by their son's poor decisions. They had no control over what he was doing, how he was wasting his inheritance, or whether he would return home. In such a situation, it seems like the parents would feel quite helpless. We don't know the backstory, but I'm confident his parents did not simply bemoan their fate. I believe they did everything they could to help the circumstance. What could they do? They could pray for their son. They could fast for him. They could strengthen their own marriage and keep their covenants. They could improve their parenting

---

[57] Shayne M. Bowen, "I Can Sleep When the Wind Blows," (Brigham Young University devotional, November 13, 2018), byu.edu/talks/shayne-m-bowen/i-can-sleep-when-wind-blows/. Accessed December 11, 2020.

skills to help their son if he returned. Above all, they could pray for strength to accept the Lord's will. Doing these things would counteract feelings of hopelessness and create feelings of determination and peace. Regardless of your circumstance, there is *always* something you can do. Find that thing, take control, and do it to the best of your ability.

Establishing a true sense of control also involves understanding our relationship with God. When we compare our meager abilities to His amazing power, we realize our efforts alone are often inadequate to deal with the challenges we face. Trying to manage life completely on our own will result in failure and frustration. We know Father in Heaven blesses us with weakness so we will be humble and turn to Him for help (see Ether 12:27). He wants us to use the power of the Savior's Atonement to strengthen our abilities. We must always do our portion, but He is ever willing to lend the strength of His mighty arm. Regarding the supporting and strengthening power of the Atonement of Jesus Christ, Elder David A. Bednar stated,

> The enabling power of the Atonement of Christ strengthens us to do things we could never do on our own. Sometimes I wonder if in our latter-day world of ease—in our world of microwave ovens and cell phones and air-conditioned cars and comfortable homes—I wonder if we ever learn to acknowledge our daily dependence upon the enabling power of the Atonement.[58]

Building a sense of control includes exercising agency in righteousness, doing difficult things, and seeking the Lord's sustaining power to strengthen our efforts. This can significantly increase our ability to cope with trials and grow stronger through difficulties. Instead of wandering aimlessly, we diligently chart a course forward and humbly accept the will of God as He directs our paths. This can create a powerful sense of confidence and a calming sense of peace when the storms come, so we can truly "sleep while the wind blows."

Thought Journal

What are two or three things you'd like to remember from this chapter?

---

[58] David A. Bednar, "In the Strength of the Lord," *BYU Speeches*, speeches.byu.edu/talks/david-a-bednar/strength-lord/. Accessed December 11, 2020.

Case Study (Sense of Control): "Stephanie"

Stephanie is a sixty-two-year-old divorced woman. She joined The Church of Jesus Christ of Latter-day Saints five years ago and has a strong testimony of the restored gospel. Stephanie has suffered from anxiety for most of her life. She remembers first noticing it when she was in middle school, suddenly becoming acutely aware of the opinions of other people around her. She worried considerably about what people thought. She felt like she constantly needed to change her clothing or hairstyle or other outward things to be accepted by others. But, generally speaking, she never did feel accepted by her peers while growing up. Her negative experiences were exacerbated while in high school. She had terrible acne, and her peers mocked her mercilessly for several years.

Although her acne cleared and the mocking stopped once she became an adult, Stephanie continued to struggle with feeling accepted by others. She would often feel intense anxiety when in social situations. As a result, she tried to avoid them as much as possible. She started a career in bookkeeping, which enabled her to be proficient at her job while not having to have much contact with others. She was able to get her work done through email and phone calls and enjoyed her solitude. When Stephanie joined the Church, she was afraid of the potential for giving talks or prayers in public. However, due to keeping a low profile, she had remained active while avoiding significant social contact. Being divorced made her feel a little odd, as there were few divorced sisters in her ward, but she did feel a sense of acceptance by ward members in general.

After many years, Stephanie went to see a counselor to talk about her concerns and was diagnosed with social anxiety disorder. This confirmed what she had known all along, but the fact that she had been formally diagnosed with a mental health condition worried her even more. What did this mean? Would she ever be able to get over it? She had always seen her anxiety as a liability, but now having a diagnosis seemed much more serious. As she approached retirement age, she looked forward to traveling the world. But would she still be able to do this? Could someone with a diagnosed anxiety disorder go to unknown places and make their way through strange lands? She worried that some of her future plans would be derailed due to her condition.

Review the three roadblocks previously discussed in this chapter (Seeing Ourselves as Objects Instead of Actors, Lack of Confidence in Our Abilities, Misunderstanding the Concept of Grace).

- In your opinion, which of these roadblocks is preventing Stephanie from moving forward? It could be one or more.

- Describe how each roadblock you have identified prevents Stephanie from progressing.

- Based on what you've learned in this chapter, what would be a helpful strategy (or strategies) for Stephanie to consider?

Resolution

Stephanie talked with her counselor about her diagnosis and possible treatment options. Her counselor reassured her that most mental health diagnoses are not permanent but can be resolved through counseling and medication. She made an appointment with her doctor and started taking medication to help with her anxiety symptoms. Stephanie continued to work with her counselor, setting a goal to develop greater social skills. Although she never reached the point of having zero anxiety in social situations, she was able to increase her ability to interact with others without fear.

Please see Appendix K for additional exercises for Chapter Eleven.

CHAPTER TWELVE
EMOTIONAL RESILIENCE ELEMENT #8:
INCREASING SPIRITUALITY

IN THEIR ARTICLE ON RESILIENCE, Connor and Davidson listed "spiritual influences" as the last of the main resilience factors.[59] This is notable, as spirituality has struggled to be recognized as a major factor in psychological studies. In many cases, it is seen as too ethereal and personal to be examined with scientific rigor. Yet as Connor and Davidson explored the outcomes of their research, they determined that one of the factors of resilience clearly aligned with this somewhat intangible concept. From a gospel perspective, it is clear that spiritual influences are critical in developing and increasing emotional resilience. That's the premise of this entire book—that gospel truth can be blended with scientific concepts to create more robust and helpful strategies to manage life's difficulties.

Science and faith have some areas of overlap while remaining largely distinct. There are times they can be used together but other times when they must be used separately. If one has a question that is purely scientific, then a scientific strategy is the best resource to find the answer. For example, if you want to see how sodium chloride is affected by water, you don't need to fast and pray about it. You can do a simple scientific experiment to find that the two ions separate when immersed. By the same token, if you want to find out if the Book of Mormon is the word of God, you don't need to explore ancient American history or excavate ruins in central Mexico. You simply need to read the book and sincerely ask God if it is true. Those who do so will receive a spiritual witness of its divinity (see Moroni 10:3–5). Developing emotional resilience can be both a scientific and spiritual process. The Lord has inspired women and men to discover truths through empirical inquiry and share them with mankind. We use those truths, combined with guidance and direction from the Holy Ghost, to improve our lives.

---

59 Connor and Davidson, "Development of a New Resilience Scale: The Connor-Davidson Resilience Scale (CD-RISC)," 76–82.

Let's reconsider the example of the brother of Jared as he struggled to find a way to light the barges he built. His solution emphasizes the partnership between secular knowledge and gospel truth. The scripture records, "And it came to pass that the brother of Jared . . . did molten out of a rock sixteen small stones; and they were white and clear, even as transparent glass" (Ether 3:1). This was long before the days of Amazon Prime, with which one might be able to order some clear stones and have them delivered in forty-eight hours. In order to fashion these stones, the brother of Jared had to either 1) use knowledge he already had or 2) get training from someone. It was a scientific process using principles of geology and fire dynamics. The Lord could have easily prepared the rocks Himself, but He wanted the brother of Jared to learn and act. With part one of the solution completed, the brother of Jared faced a roadblock. There were no existing technologies to make a rock glow. Having done his part, he turned to the Lord for help.

> And I know, O Lord, that thou hast all power, and can do whatsoever thou wilt for the benefit of man; therefore touch these stones, O Lord, with thy finger, and prepare them that they may shine forth in darkness. (Ether 3:4)

The premortal Jesus Christ put forth His hand and caused the stones to glow. Can you see the partnership? The brother of Jared did his part; the Lord did His. As you work to develop greater emotional resilience, can you understand that you need to do your portion to the best of your ability and then rely on heavenly strength to accomplish the rest? We cannot do it all ourselves, nor can we leave it all to the Lord. We must work together.

Learning to develop emotional resilience, especially with all its components, can be a difficult and lifelong process. Motivation can be hard to maintain. To remain driven toward your goal, you'll have to discover your own sense of purpose. I cannot provide it for you. Even if I could, I wouldn't. Each of us needs to decide why we choose to live the gospel and follow the Savior. But once we become converted to the idea of progression, our motivation is strengthened. We start to view progress as positive and beneficial, worth the sacrifices made to obtain it. But if we only change because someone else wants us to or because we see it as a required but pointless task, then our motivation may be weak.

The war chapters of the Book of Mormon contain valuable insights regarding our mortal journey. They are much more than just interesting stories. In many ways, they are allegories regarding our current fight against sin. When

Captain Moroni took charge of the Nephite armies, he disrupted the status quo. Through innovation and revelation, he found new ways of warfare that gave his people the advantage over the Lamanites. One of these innovations was protective armor. In one of his first battles with the Lamanites, Moroni's armies showed up clothed from head to toe with helmets, breastplates, shields, and thick clothing. The Lamanites came in their usual fashion: naked except for a loincloth. You can imagine the outcome. The Nephite armies began to decimate their enemies. One might assume that the contest would have been extremely lopsided and quickly ended, but not so. Notwithstanding their exposure, the Lamanites "[fought] like dragons" (Alma 43:44). Their fierceness and intensity were surprising and even frightening to the Nephites, and to some extent, the Nephites' resolve began to wane. When faced with a truly formidable foe, notwithstanding their own armor, they wanted to retreat.

Is this familiar to you? Are there times when you want to change, make a great first effort, but find yourself abandoning the cause after a short time? I imagine most everyone has had such an experience. If you have, don't worry. It is a very common condition and nothing to be ashamed of. Successful improvement is almost always an iterative process that involves some steps forward, some steps backward, and periodic rests. You might have the same experience while reading this book. After reading it through, you might say, "I'm going to do it! I'm going to put in the work to develop greater emotional resilience." You create action plans and set a course for change. Then when the road gets steeper, or when opposing forces intensify, you wonder if you have the grit to continue. You wonder if it's even worth it. Before you chastise yourself for such thinking, rest assured that this is extremely common and part of being human. You are not alone in such thoughts. However, that does not mean you have to succumb to them. You can receive extra strength to endure and prevail. Let's return to the Nephites' story and find out how they coped with their difficult situation.

> And it came to pass that when the men of Moroni saw the fierceness and the anger of the Lamanites, they were about to shrink and flee from them. And Moroni, perceiving their intent, sent forth and inspired their hearts with these thoughts—yea, the thoughts of their lands, their liberty, yea, their freedom from bondage. (Alma 43:48)

Captain Moroni reminded his armies of their purpose. He reminded them of the reason they came to battle in the first place and what was on the line if they failed. He didn't threaten them. Threats have very little long-term power to motivate. Rather, he inspired them with thoughts of what they truly valued. He helped them remember their goal and that their objective was worth the fight. We all need a cheerleader like Captain Moroni. Perhaps this can be a friend, sibling, spouse, church leader, ministering sister or brother, or mental health professional. You may have to do your part to seek out such help. If you don't feel like you have access to such resources, the Lord will always be your cheerleader no matter what. Such supports can help us keep perspective when our vision clouds and our motivation declines.

And what was the effect of Captain Moroni's encouragement?

> And it came to pass that they turned upon the Lamanites, *and they cried with one voice unto the Lord their God*, for their liberty and their freedom from bondage. *And they began to stand against the Lamanites with power; and in that selfsame hour that they cried unto the Lord for their freedom, the Lamanites began to flee before them.* (Alma 43:49–50; emphases added)

When the Nephites remembered the value of what they were doing and the potential blessings that awaited them, they did two things. First, they sought heavenly help. They asked for strength to achieve their righteous goal. Second, they acted. They "stood against the Lamanites with power." What was the power? It was a hybrid of their own efforts and the strength of the Lord. As we have discussed previously, the Lord rarely fights our battles completely for us. He doesn't relegate us to the sidelines while He scores touchdown after touchdown against our adversary. Rather, He keeps us in the game while providing excellent coaching and additional strength and sometimes even joins the huddle for a play or two. When we play, we learn. When we work, we grow. We were never intended to do it all on our own, but neither were we to surrender the responsibility of our progression to another. As you strive to develop greater emotional resilience, you'll need God's help. You will also need to get in the game and put forth your best efforts, the best you can muster on any given day, particularly when the going gets tough.

The Nephites were inspired by thoughts of preserving their freedom, their lands, the safety of their families, and their right to worship God. What will inspire you? What is the motivation that will keep you going during challenges? The answers are very individual, and for the most part, you can discover them for yourself. However, there are certain principles that apply to all of Father in

Heaven's children that can help inspire us to move forward. Pressing forward on the covenant path requires obedience. Although obedience is difficult, it was never intended to be an onerous chore. As we've previously discussed, moral agency is an amazing gift. Satan, ever jealous of our potential for progress, encourages our misuse of agency. He claims that commandments somehow curtail our freedom of choice. He whispers, "God gave you agency but demands you use it in a certain way? That seems backward. It seems restricting. You shouldn't have to choose anything you don't want to; that's the whole point of freedom of choice." As with many of Satan's temptations, he uses elements of truth along with lies. Consider the example of Eve, when Satan tempted her to partake of the forbidden fruit. He said, "Ye shall not surely die; For God doth know that in the day ye eat thereof, then your eyes shall be opened, and ye shall be as gods, knowing good and evil" (Moses 4:10–11). The *truth* was that her eyes would be opened. The *lie* was that she would not die.

Regarding obedience, the *truth* is we don't have to choose something we don't want to. God does not force our choices. The *lie* is that obedience to commandments is restricting. *It is not.* Many who have strayed from the straight and narrow path can testify that they were more restricted during their sinful journey than when following the Lord's path. This is one of the glorious, paradoxical truths of the gospel. When we make a sacrifice of agency to follow God's commands, we discover greater freedom than ever before.

Freedom and strength are not the only outcomes of obedience. Those who truly follow the Savior can experience great joy in their daily walk. They are free from the shackles of sin and the misery of disobedience. Their journey home can become one of happiness and anticipation. This takes effort and sometimes requires needed attitude adjustments. Obedience shows love for Heavenly Father and allows us to feel His love more abundantly. Carol M. Stephens, former First Counselor in the Relief Society General Presidency, taught this principle:

> We may feel at times that God's laws restrict our personal freedom, take from us our agency, and limit our growth. But as we seek for greater understanding, as we allow our Father to teach us, we will begin to see that His laws are a manifestation of His love for us and obedience to His laws is an expression of our love for Him.[60]

---

60 Carol M. Stephens, "If Ye Love Me, Keep My Commandments," *Ensign*, November 2015, 119.

Our walk back to Father in Heaven was never designed to be miserable. Although it necessarily must be filled with challenges and tests, we can find peace in the journey. Key facets to emotional resilience include understanding the purpose of trials, accepting them as a critical piece of our development, and doing our best to face them with resolve and determination. Perhaps that is what Connor and Davidson were attempting to describe with the idea of "spiritual influences."[61] Knowing there is something greater than ourselves and that we are part of an eternal, personalized plan can provide great strength to persist and grow during difficult times.

In the closing chapters of the Book of Mormon, Moroni includes a transcript of an address given by Mormon to the Nephite saints. Mormon introduces his comments as follows:

> Wherefore, I would speak unto you that are of the church, that are the *peaceable followers of Christ*, and that have obtained a sufficient hope by which ye can enter into the rest of the Lord, from this time henceforth until ye shall rest with him in heaven. And now my brethren, I judge these things of you because of *your peaceable walk* with the children of men. (Moroni 7:3–4; emphases added)

I'm intrigued by the word *peaceable*. Mormon uses it twice: once to describe the followers of the Savior and once to describe their interactions with others. What does it mean? Why use that particular word to describe the character and behavior of the Savior's disciples? Jesus told his Apostles, "Peace I leave with you, my peace I give unto you: *not as the world giveth, give I unto you*" (John 14:27; emphasis added). His statement seems to clearly establish a difference between the world's version of peace and His version. So what is the difference?

I think the difference can be summarized with the concepts of "external" versus "internal" peace. The world's peace is defined by objective, observable peace. It is manifest in plentiful harvests, cease-fires, and calm seas. Once the winds kick up or conflicts resume, the world's peace is destroyed. In one's own life, the world's peace is often represented by happy families, secure employment, and abundant living. As long as no one rocks the boat, the world's peace prevails. The Savior's peace is defined by an internal and eternal perspective.

---

[61] Connor and Davidson, "Development of a New Resilience Scale: The Connor-Davidson Resilience Scale (CD-RISC)," 76–82.

It provides comfort regardless of the external experience. The Savior's peace allowed Him to sleep on a boat during a tempest (see Matthew 8:24). It allowed Joseph Smith to face his impending martyrdom "calm as a summer's morning" (D&C 135:4). That same peace enables us to be confident during times of trial and hopeful during times of uncertainty. Regarding emotional resilience, the "peaceable walk" is a self-assured, optimistic walk. It is a walk that, notwithstanding present difficulties, looks forward with faith. As we develop greater emotional resilience, we increase our ability to move along the covenant path with grit and determination, accepting challenges and using them to become more like the Savior.

Consider Lehi's vision of the tree of life. Those who were successful in reaching the tree and not falling away were described as "continually holding fast to the rod of iron" (1 Nephi 8:30). They endured the mists of darkness and came out stronger on the other side. In his discourse to the ancient Nephites, Mormon talks about "laying hold" of good things: "And now I come to that faith, of which I said I would speak; and I will tell you the way whereby ye may *lay hold on every good thing*" (Moroni 7:21; emphasis added). I think it is no coincidence that Lehi saw faithful disciples "holding fast" to the gospel and Mormon described faith as "laying hold" of principles that will help us become more like the Savior. Emotional resilience is greatly enhanced by faith. Picture yourself as one of the countless people in Lehi's dream. You see the tree in the distance and want to get there. You press forward, grabbing the iron rod, and begin your journey. Then the mists of darkness come. They are disorienting. They are persistent. They completely prevent your view of the tree. Moving forward becomes more difficult. As you tread forward, step by step, in the confusing darkness, you start to wonder why you are doing it. Is the tree still there, even though you can't see it? Is it worth the stress and effort to continue?

Or what if you find yourself nowhere close to the rod of iron? Perhaps you feel you have been deceived by those in the great and spacious building and are inching your way toward that edifice. Perhaps you have begun to wander along strange roads, feeling lost. What can you do? Is the rod and the resilience that comes from holding fast beyond your grasp? No! We can always change direction; that's the beauty of the Savior's Atonement. Just start where you are. Turn around, face the tree of life, and start heading in that direction. Satan would have us believe that our case is beyond hope; *he is a liar*. Listen to the comforting, encouraging whispers of the Spirit. He will help you change course, move forward, and begin to experience the joy of heading toward greater happiness.

This is why faith is so critical as we endure challenges. Moroni taught,

> I would show unto the world that faith is things which are hoped for and not seen; wherefore, dispute not because ye see not, for ye receive no witness until after the trial of your faith. (Ether 12:6)

Just because you can't see the tree of life through the mists of darkness doesn't mean it isn't there. *It is there.* Just because you have lost your way and are unsure the tree will bring you joy doesn't mean it won't. *It will.* As life is a test, we must have times in which we cannot clearly see our destination. Pretty much everyone who sees the tree of life recognizes its potential for happiness; it is magnificent and desirable. That's not the test. The test comes when we can no longer see it; then what? Do we still have faith it is there? Do we still believe our efforts to endure will be rewarded? Faith keeps us going during times of stress. It helps us see grander outcomes that encourage ongoing diligence.

Chapter Twelve Exercise

Here is an opportunity for you to examine something specific in your life, to determine possible strategies to help you increase your spiritual capacity.

Reflect on Lehi's description of "continually holding fast" and Mormon's discussion of "laying hold on every good thing."

- What are things you can do to grasp on to or better hold on to the iron rod? List at least three.

- Consider the three things you described above. Which one of them are you the least diligent at? In other words, which one of them could you improve the most?

- Regarding the one thing you noted above, devise a simple plan to improve your performance in that area. Write your plan here:

Mormon speaks of the power of faith as it relates to our ability to accomplish righteous goals: "And Christ hath said: If ye will have faith in me ye shall have power to do whatsoever thing is expedient in me" (Moroni 7:33). We will receive heavenly help with goals that are "expedient" in Him. Is it "expedient in Christ" that you overcome your challenges, develop greater emotional strength, and become the type of person who can endure stress with more success? I believe so. The Lord's own description of His purpose supports my belief: "For behold, this is my work and my glory—to bring to pass the immortality and eternal life of man" (Moses 1:39). His work and His glory are to have us become like Him. We are to walk a path similar to His. It is one of strain, endurance, and ultimate triumph. It helps us meet the measure of our creation. With that in mind, it seems obvious that He would give us the power described by Mormon to help us achieve this most expedient of goals. Developing emotional resilience is within our reach as we seek the Lord's help and strength to accomplish our goals.

Mormon continues his teachings as he highlights the doctrine of hope, which is a companion principle to faith. Hope is often less understood and does not get as much attention as faith, but this principle is critical to understand and apply. Faith is a belief and knowledge that something is true. Hope attaches a feeling of joyful anticipation to that same truth. Consider the difference between these two statements: "I *hope* to serve a mission someday" and "I *believe* I'll serve a mission someday." The second statement connotes belief in a likely truth (faith), but it seems void of emotion. It is a simple statement of fact. "I *believe* the Church's mission program exists and that, in time, they will likely ask me to participate." But what of the first statement, wherein hope is referenced? Not only does it express the fact that the mission program exists and a call to serve is possible but it also suggests an eagerness and expectation that is absent in the other statement. It says, "I really want to be a missionary. I look forward to that day. I *hope* I can be part of that grand program." Hope builds on faith and creates an emotional connection to the belief. In doing that, it strengthens commitment. Returning to the example of the multitudes trying to reach the tree of life, consider these companion motivations: *I believe I can make it to the tree* versus *I hope I can make it to the tree*. They are both essential but offer differing supports. One provides the desire to get moving in the first place, and the other provides ongoing motivation to continue when the going gets tough.

Hope can be a light in the darkness. It can buoy our spirits when waves of adversity come crashing down. Emotional resilience is the power to persist through difficulty. I suppose one can persist without hope, but doing so becomes a miserable grind. When someone has something good to look forward to, enduring trials can become more joyful. I believe this is what Alma the Younger meant when he taught to "look forward with an eye of faith" (Alma 5:15). Surely, we can also look forward with an eye of hope. Regarding Lehi's dream, we keep our eyes focused on the tree of life. When mists of darkness dim our mortal sight, our eyes of faith and hope still see clearly and help us move forward with determination. Elaine S. Dalton, former Young Women General President, taught,

> The Savior is not only the light and life of the world; He is our one bright hope. Through Him you can have the hope of returning to live with your Father in Heaven. Through Him you can repent and overcome the things that will keep you from being steadfast. Through Him you can find the strength and courage to press forward even when the winds of resistance blow.[62]

Thought Journal

What are two or three things you'd like to remember from this chapter?

Please see Appendix L for additional exercises for Chapter Twelve.

---

[62] Elaine S. Dalton, "Press Forward and Be Steadfast," *Ensign*, May 2003, 107.

Conclusion

My dear friends, please understand that your lives will be difficult by design. An all-knowing, all-loving Father in Heaven is in charge. Although He will help you navigate difficulties, His ultimate ambitions for you are much grander. He is trying to transform you into something completely different. He wants you to become a new creature, fashioned after His celestial image, complete with all His magnificent and glorious characteristics. *This process takes time and effort.* The roadblocks you encounter are not obstructions but opportunities for growth and development. Greater emotional resilience will enable you to push forward, overcoming barrier upon barrier, gaining strength through your journey. The process is as refining as it is grueling. Don't despair. The Lord counseled the pioneer saints, who were no strangers to the need for emotional resilience, with the following encouragement: "Wherefore, be not weary in well-doing, for ye are laying the foundation of a great work. And out of small things proceedeth that which is great" (D&C 64:33).

Remember these principles as you try to apply the teachings in this book. "Be not weary in well-doing" (D&C 64:33). In other words, don't give up. Don't stop after initial frustrations or failures. As you continue to work toward change, you will find the process becomes easier and more familiar. "Out of small things proceedeth that which is great" (D&C 64:33). Take small steps. Break large goals into manageable activities. Do something every day to build your emotional resilience, even if it seems insignificant. In time, those small, simple things will yield amazing results. Finally, remember "ye are laying the foundation of a great work" (D&C 64:33). You came to Earth for something great. Your eternal destiny is incredible, and it is built upon the foundation of your daily effort combined with the Savior's redeeming power. You are a child of the Everlasting God, and He will preserve and sustain you, magnifying your strength as you diligently and sincerely seek His help. As the Lord taught so long ago,

> Therefore whosoever heareth these sayings of mine, and doeth them, I will liken him unto a wise man, which built his house upon a rock: And the rain descended, and the floods came, and the winds blew, and beat upon that house; and it fell not: for it was founded upon a rock. (Matthew 7:24–25)

God bless you to weather such storms well.

APPENDICES

Remember, realistic goals are typically specific and achievable. Large goals often need to be broken down into smaller goals in order to ultimately be met. Goals should stretch you past your current level of comfort but not be so extreme that they are constantly frustrating. Reflect on the counsel in 2 Nephi 28:30 as you prayerfully establish your personal plan.

APPENDIX A

Chapter One Summary

Righteous behavior does not prevent mortal suffering. Trials and difficulties can be effective teachers if endured well. Emotional resilience is the ability not only to endure adversity but to thrive in it as well. From a spiritual perspective, the challenges we face in life help us refine ourselves spiritually and become more like our Father in Heaven.

Questions to Consider

- Consider a significant trial you've experienced. In what ways did it test your faith? In what ways did it build your faith?

- How can an increase in personal afflictions represent God's love for and confidence in you?

- What other questions have come to your mind as you've read this chapter?

Scriptures to Study

- What insights come to your mind as you ponder these verses?

Behold, I have refined thee, but not with silver; I have chosen thee in the furnace of affliction. (Isaiah 48:10)

And above all, if the very jaws of hell shall gape open the mouth wide after thee, know thou, my son, that all these things shall give thee experience, and shall be for thy good. (D&C 122:7)

- Using footnotes and other scripture study helps, what additional scriptures can you find that relate to the insights you've had as you've read this chapter?

My Personal Plan

- What can I do to create greater faith in the Father's plan for me?

- How will I measure my progress as I develop this skill?

- List any other personal goals related to insights you've had while studying this chapter.

APPENDIX B

Chapter Two Summary

Trials come from many sources. Sometimes trials come from our Father in Heaven. The purpose of these trials is to help us grow closer to Him and become more spiritually refined. The process of disruption helps break us down so we can be rebuilt into something stronger and more resilient.

Questions to Consider

- Consider a significant disruption in your life. How did it provide opportunities for personal growth?

- What are some things you can do to more humbly accept the will of your Father in Heaven?

- What other questions have come to your mind as you've read this chapter?

Scriptures to Study

- What insights come to your mind as you ponder these verses?

    Peace be unto thy soul; thine adversity and thine afflictions shall be but a small moment; And then, if thou endure it well, God shall exalt thee on high. (D&C 121:7–8)

For after much tribulation come the blessings. Wherefore the day cometh that ye shall be crowned with much glory; the hour is not yet, but is nigh at hand. (D&C 58:4)

- Using footnotes and other scripture study helps, what additional scriptures can you find that relate to the insights you've had as you've read this chapter?

My Personal Plan

- What can I do to respond positively to disruptive events?

- How will I measure my progress as I develop this skill?

- List any other personal goals related to insights you've had while studying this chapter.

APPENDIX C

Chapter Three Summary

An understanding of our identity and purpose can help us develop greater emotional resilience. It is critical to be intentional about this process. We can become distracted by both good and bad things that decrease our progress. The example of Moses's visit from God and his subsequent temptation by Satan teaches that understanding identity and purpose builds spiritual and emotional strength.

Questions to Consider

- What is your identity? How does understanding your divine identity help you remain on the covenant path?

- What is your purpose? How does understanding your eternal purpose provide motivation to endure trials?

- What other questions have come to your mind as you've read this chapter?

Scriptures to Study

- What insights come to your mind as you ponder these verses?

    Whereby are given unto us exceeding great and precious promises: that by these ye might be partakers of the divine nature, having escaped the corruption that is in the world through lust. (2 Peter 1:4)

    Verily I say, men should be anxiously engaged in a good cause, and do many things of their own free will, and bring to pass much righteousness; For the power is in them, wherein they are agents unto themselves. And inasmuch as men do good they shall in nowise lose their reward. (D&C 58:27–28)

- Using footnotes and other scripture study helps, what additional scriptures can you find that relate to the insights you've had as you've read this chapter?

My Personal Plan

- What can I do to better understand my identity and purpose?

- How will I measure my progress as I develop this skill?

- List any other personal goals related to insights you've had while studying this chapter.

APPENDIX D

Chapter Four Summary

Spiritual help from God is essential in solving problems and coping with stress, but that does not mean we don't have a part to play. The Atonement of Jesus Christ provides strength and support to help us do our portion. Because trials are essential for our development, we should seek for strength to endure rather than for trials to be erased.

Questions to Consider

- How have you experienced the enabling power of the Savior's Atonement in your life?

- What are some areas in your life where you can pray for strength to endure and improve?

- What other questions have come to your mind as you've read this chapter?

Scriptures to Study

- What insights come to your mind as you ponder these verses?

For we have not an high priest which cannot be touched with the feeling of our infirmities; but was in all points tempted like as we are, yet without sin. (Hebrews 4:15)

And now it came to pass that the burdens which were laid upon Alma and his brethren were made light; yea, the Lord did strengthen them that they could bear up their burdens with ease, and they did submit cheerfully and with patience to all the will of the Lord. (Mosiah 24:15)

- Using footnotes and other scripture study helps, what additional scriptures can you find that relate to the insights you've had as you've read this chapter?

My Personal Plan

- What can I do to receive the enabling power of the Atonement of Jesus Christ in my life?

- How will I measure my progress as I develop this skill?

- List any other personal goals related to insights you've had while studying this chapter.

APPENDIX E

Chapter Five Summary

Personal competence is the belief in one's ability to set and achieve goals. Setting appropriate and righteous goals can help us move forward and develop a sense of purpose. We can overcome roadblocks to goals by having self-confidence and increasing our faith in the Lord's ability to help us move along the covenant path.

Questions to Consider

- How would you rate your ability to set and achieve goals?

- What are some things you could do to improve your self-confidence?

- What other questions have come to your mind as you've read this chapter?

Scriptures to Study

- What insights come to your mind as you ponder these verses?

    For of him unto whom much is given much is required; and he who sins against the greater light shall receive the greater condemnation. (D&C 82:3)

I can do all things through Christ which strengtheneth me. (Philippians 4:13)

- Using footnotes and other scripture study helps, what additional scriptures can you find that relate to the insights you've had as you've read this chapter?

My Personal Plan

- What can I do to improve my ability to set and achieve goals?

- How will I measure my progress as I develop this skill?

- List any other personal goals related to insights you've had while studying this chapter.

APPENDIX F

Chapter Six Summary

Tenacity is being determined and persistent, continuing to move forward despite obstacles. False dilemmas can create barriers to tenacity but can be overcome through flexible thinking and asking for heavenly help. Developing tenacity can help us endure to the end and increase in spiritual strength.

Questions to Consider

- How would you rate your ability to persist in the face of challenges?

- As you consider the future, do you tend to have a more positive or more negative outlook? What are some things you can do to strengthen a more positive outlook?

- What other questions have come to your mind as you've read this chapter?

Scriptures to Study

- What insights come to your mind as you ponder these verses?

    For we are made partakers of Christ, if we hold the beginning of our confidence steadfast unto the end. (Hebrews 3:14)

> Now this was a great trial to those that did stand fast in the faith; nevertheless, they were steadfast and immovable in keeping the commandments of God, and they bore with patience the persecution which was heaped upon them. (Alma 1:25)

- Using footnotes and other scripture study helps, what additional scriptures can you find that relate to the insights you've had as you've read this chapter?

My Personal Plan

- What can I do to improve my skill of tenacity?

- How will I measure my progress as I develop this skill?

- List any other personal goals related to insights you've had while studying this chapter.

APPENDIX G

Chapter Seven Summary

Learning to see stress as a potential tool for growth is helpful. Trying to avoid all stress is ineffective and unproductive. As we learn to accept that stress can help us move forward, we will gain greater strength and develop stronger faith.

Questions to Consider

- In what ways can stressful situations be a blessing to you personally?

- How can viewing certain trials as part of the Father's plan help you develop greater faith in Him?

- What other questions have come to your mind as you've read this chapter?

Scriptures to Study

- What insights come to your mind as you ponder these verses?

    Then said Jesus unto his disciples, If any man will come after me, let him deny himself, and take up his cross, and follow me. (Matthew 16:24)

> Therefore I take pleasure in infirmities, in reproaches, in necessities, in persecutions, in distresses for Christ's sake: for when I am weak, then am I strong. (2 Corinthians 12:10)

- Using footnotes and other scripture study helps, what additional scriptures can you find that relate to the insights you've had as you've read this chapter?

My Personal Plan

- What can I do to see stressful situations as a growth opportunity?

- How will I measure my progress as I develop this skill?

- List any other personal goals related to insights you've had while studying this chapter.

APPENDIX H

Chapter Eight Summary

Tolerance of negative affect refers to the degree to which we are willing to tolerate, or endure, negative feelings or emotions. If we try to escape all negative emotions, we will never develop the strength needed to face them effectively. Resiliently enduring challenging situations can help us be better prepared to handle future adversity.

Questions to Consider

- How can learning to tolerate negative emotions help you become more like the Savior?

- What help do you need to face challenges with greater determination?

- What other questions have come to your mind as you've read this chapter?

Scriptures to Study

- What insights come to your mind as you ponder these verses?

    And whoso taketh upon him my name, and endureth to the end, the same shall be saved at the last day. (3 Nephi 27:6)

He that is faithful and endureth shall overcome the world. (D&C 63:47)

- Using footnotes and other scripture study helps, what additional scriptures can you find that relate to the insights you've had as you've read this chapter?

My Personal Plan

- What can I do to develop stronger tolerance of negative feelings?

- How will I measure my progress as I develop this skill?

- List any other personal goals related to insights you've had while studying this chapter.

APPENDIX I

Chapter Nine Summary

Change is practically constant in our lives but is something that many struggle to accept. When we resist change, we often limit our capacity for growth. The gospel of Jesus Christ is a vehicle of change, helping us become like our Father in Heaven. As we accept change as positive and use it to our benefit, we develop greater emotional resilience.

Questions to Consider

- Generally speaking, how well do you adapt to changes in your life?

- What can you do to increase your faith in Jesus Christ and His power to sustain you through unexpected changes?

- What other questions have come to your mind as you've read this chapter?

Scriptures to Study

- What insights come to your mind as you ponder these verses?

    Trust in the Lord with all thine heart; and lean not unto thine own understanding. In all thy ways acknowledge him, and he shall direct thy paths. (Proverbs 3:5–6)

> For I do know that whosoever shall put their trust in God shall be supported in their trials, and their troubles, and their afflictions, and shall be lifted up at the last day. (Alma 36:3)

- Using footnotes and other scripture study helps, what additional scriptures can you find that relate to the insights you've had as you've read this chapter?

My Personal Plan

- What can I do to develop a greater ability to tolerate changes?

- How will I measure my progress as I develop this skill?

- List any other personal goals related to insights you've had while studying this chapter.

APPENDIX J

Chapter Ten Summary

Having secure relationships is critical to developing emotional strength. We need to have strong earthly relationships with each other as well as strong relationships with our Father in Heaven and Jesus Christ. Forging a solid relationship with God and the Savior is critical in our eternal progression.

Questions to Consider

- How can you show greater love and understanding toward those you disagree with?

- What can you do to improve your relationship with your Father in Heaven?

- What other questions have come to your mind as you've read this chapter?

Scriptures to Study

- What insights come to your mind as you ponder these verses?

    A friend loveth at all times, and a brother is born for adversity. (Proverbs 17:17)

> Thus did Alma teach his people, that every man should love his neighbor as himself, that there should be no contention among them. (Mosiah 23:15)

- Using footnotes and other scripture study helps, what additional scriptures can you find that relate to the insights you've had as you've read this chapter?

My Personal Plan

- What can I do to build securer relationships with others?

- How will I measure my progress as I develop this skill?

- List any other personal goals related to insights you've had while studying this chapter.

APPENDIX K

Chapter Eleven Summary

Developing a healthy sense of control is crucial to emotional resilience. The gift of moral agency is both the ability and responsibility to make good choices. As we access the power of the Savior's Atonement, we increase our ability to do our portion and understand how to rely on His strength.

Questions to Consider

- Think about a current problem you face. What can you do in order to take more accountability and increase healthy control in this situation?

- What personal changes can you make to see yourself more as a person to act as opposed to a person to be acted upon?

- What other questions have come to your mind as you've read this chapter?

Scriptures to Study

- What insights come to your mind as you ponder these verses?

    He hath given unto you that ye might know good from evil, and he hath given unto you that ye might choose life or death; and ye can do good and be restored unto that which is good, or have that which is good restored unto you; or ye can do evil, and have that which is evil restored unto you. (Helaman 14:31)

And it is given unto them to know good from evil; wherefore they are agents unto themselves, and I have given unto you another law and commandment. (Moses 6:56)

- Using footnotes and other scripture study helps, what additional scriptures can you find that relate to the insights you've had as you've read this chapter?

My Personal Plan

- What can I do to increase a healthy sense of control in my life?

- How will I measure my progress as I develop this skill?

- List any other personal goals related to insights you've had while studying this chapter.

APPENDIX L

Chapter Twelve Summary

To effectively face challenges, we must use a combination of our own efforts and heavenly help. Developing a solid testimony of truth can help us remain motivated to do what's right during times of weakness and despair. Although life will be difficult, hope will provide a light to shine throughout dark days.

Questions to Consider

- What is your understanding of the difference between faith and hope? What can you do to increase your faith? What can you do to increase your hope?

- How can you better "look forward with an eye of faith" (Alma 5:15) when trials become difficult?

- What other questions have come to your mind as you've read this chapter?

Scriptures to Study

- What insights come to your mind as you ponder these verses?

> Having faith on the Lord; having a hope that ye shall receive eternal life; having the love of God always in your hearts, that ye may be lifted up at the last day and enter into his rest. (Alma 13:29)

> Now the God of hope fill you with all joy and peace in believing, that ye may abound in hope, through the power of the Holy Ghost. (Romans 15:13)

- Using footnotes and other scripture study helps, what additional scriptures can you find that relate to the insights you've had as you've read this chapter?

My Personal Plan

- What can I do to improve my relationship with Heavenly Father and Jesus Christ?

- How will I measure my progress as I develop this skill?

- List any other personal goals related to insights you've had while studying this chapter.

ABOUT THE AUTHOR

DAVID T. MORGAN IS A graduate of Brigham Young University with a doctorate in counseling psychology. He has worked as a psychologist in private practice for almost twenty years. Over thirty years ago he married his best friend, and they have six children together, in addition to several daughters-in-law and multiple grandchildren. Dr. Morgan is the author of five books on gospel and mental health topics, a regular presenter with Onward Productions, and a contributing author to *LDS Living* magazine. He was a presenter at the 2021 BYU Women's Conference and 2021 BYU Education Week. He is convinced that the gospel of Jesus Christ holds multiple keys to improving emotional and mental health. His favorite hobby is going to Disneyland, and he has been over one hundred times.

Visit Dr. Morgan's website at drdavidmorgan.com, or follow him on social media.

Instagram: @dr_davidmorgan
Facebook: facebook.com/davidtmorganphd